Motherly Advice From Cathy's Mom

Anne Guisewite

Motherly Advice From Cathy's Mom

With illustrations by my beautiful and talented daughter, Cathy Guisewite

Andrews, McMeel & Parker / A Universal Press Syndicate Affiliate

KANSAS CITY / NEW YORK

ISBN: 0-8362-2091-9
Library of Congress Catalog Card Number: 86-72793

Contents

Foreword

My mother and I have the kind of special relationship that so many mothers and daughters share: First I beg her for advice, then I scream at her for giving it. The only thing more annoying than having her tell me for the hundredth time how to get the grime off the shower curtain is to discover that, for the 101st time, I've forgotten how to do it.

We thought maybe she should write some of this down. Not only would it save her from repeating herself, but it would give me the chance to seek and reject her opinion without her actually having to be in the same room.

It's all part of an incredible mother/daughter duet that goes on from the moment we first pledge we will be nothing like our mothers, up to and including the moment their words start pouring out of our own mouths.

Needless to say, anyone who's ever wondered if the mother in the comic strip is anything like my own will get some real insight into the wealth of love, devotion, and "sensible suggestions" I've had to draw on all this time.

You may read this and be filled with warmth because it sounds exactly like your mother. You may read it and get a stomachache because it sounds exactly like your mother. You may read it and say, "Hah! That's nothing compared to what mine comes up with!"

Whatever your reaction, I'll bet that some frazzled evening, when dinner is smoldering in the kitchen, your business associates are comatose in the living room, and the outfit you're wearing is shrinking right before your eyes, you'll find some comfort in sneaking into a corner, flipping through the pages, and having someone's mom not only tell you you're doing just fine, but that almost anything could be fixed with a little vinegar.

—CATHY GUISEWITE

Dear Cathy,

When you asked me to jot down some advice on housekeeping and "stuff," you never dreamed you'd get an avalanche in reply, did you? Well, neither did I.

The more I thought about it, though, the more the advice just kept spilling out. I may have digressed a bit here and there, but aren't mothers entitled to some parental license? After all, as one popular commercial suggested, "We've earned it."

Thanks, Cathy, for inviting me to speak my piece and then bringing it to life with your cartoons. And thanks, too, to Andrews, McMeel & Parker for publishing it.

Love,

Mom

1   Housekeeping

Your apartment is lovely, sweetie. You've filled it with the kind of junk your father and I couldn't wait to get rid of as soon as we could afford some nice furniture. We gave ours away to whatever charitable organization was willing to pick it up. You've rediscovered it in flea markets and eclectic emporiums at outlandish prices over which Dad and I can only shake our heads, while we admire how cleverly and attractively you've put it to use. (Would you believe that the reaction of our parents was hauntingly similar?)

Congratulations on doing it all by yourself with nobody to help you pay for it, lug it in, and put everything in place. I couldn't have done it alone and am bursting with admiration and pride that you did. You modern young women are an inspiration to your mothers.

But, have you noticed, now that it's your home, that if you drop something, there it stays until you pick it up? That if you dirty it, you must clean it or hire someone else to? That if you break it, you must fix or replace it? That if you own it, you must take care of it? Welcome to housekeeping, Cathy.

It has taken me forty years to learn a few things about this job the hard way. I'm sure it won't take you anywhere near that long. May I suggest a few tips?

In order to find what you need when you need it, you must put it back after you have used it. Unfortunately, this is one of the things you never learned very well from your mother. Maybe that's because it's not one of her specialties, either. Practice it, though, as you used to practice piano until it becomes a mechanical reflex. It may take years to perfect, but it's worth the effort.

Keep a sponge and cake of soap by the sink to wipe up spills promptly before they settle in as stains. This is also a good way to whisk a dish or coffee cup out of sight. It's more aesthetic than letting a sinkful accumulate.

Baking soda and vinegar are fine cleaning products, and they're cheap. Baking soda works well on any porcelain-finish surface—refrigerators, stoves, even teeth. Blend it into a paste or dissolve it in water. Vinegar (about a cup in a quart of water) makes windows sparkle—especially if you dry them with crumpled newspapers. Wipe up and down on the inside of the pane and across on the outside, and you'll know which side the streak is on. Usually, I use white vinegar, not because it cleans any better, but because it is multipurpose. It can help rinse soap out of laundry and shampoo out of hair, set color in new garments, and release stains from the armpits and hemlines of clothes, as well as be useful in cooking.

Are your shower curtains getting grimy and spotted? Scrub them with a brush dipped in vinegar. Fill clogged steam irons and coffee pots with vinegar, steam it through, then steam through some fresh water before using. Copper turning black? A paste of vinegar, salt, and flour (equal amounts of flour and salt plus enough vinegar to give it the consistency of thick ketchup) will brighten almost like new. (Keep vinegar away from your cast-iron skillets, though; it rusts them.) Mop your floor with vinegar water (same strength as for windows) to disinfect and clean it at the same time. Vinegar is not only for salads, you'll find, if you ever get over your aversion to the way it smells. Of course I use commercial cleaners, too. So will you. But they're not the only way to clean.

Let me introduce you to ammonia. Another good cleaner and disinfectant, ammonia works best alone. Never mix it with bleach, the fumes could knock you out. And the color effect! I mixed them once in the washing machine and the armpits on Dad's dazzling white shirts turned permanently bright orange. Wearing rubber gloves, pour some ammonia on a sponge and wipe off the toilet seat and floor to disinfect.

Too many young women are intimidated by chlorine bleach. Too bad. With a little perseverance, you can make bleach your slave. In the laundry, it is capable of lifting spots, brightening brights (one-half cup per tubful, well-diluted), and whitening whites (one to two cups per load, depending on soil). It will also whiten the blackened grout around your bathroom tiles and tub and lift embedded grime out of the linoleum. Don't wear your favorite jeans or sweater when you're working with it.

But, doll, if you master nothing else in housekeeping, master the flying five-minute pickup. It will save your sanity, sweeten your disposition, do wonders for your morale, and establish your reputation as a housekeeper.

To accomplish it, borrow five minutes from your usual wake-up time or your shampoo/shower or wherever you can nudge your schedule a bit. Use these five minutes this way:

Before you walk out of any room in your apartment, put every out-of-place object in that room where it belongs. Or, at least put it in a container to be dealt with when you return home. Do the same with the next room you step into, then the next, working your way out. It can make the difference between loving where you live or hating it.

The secret is to really fly—your eyes darting everywhere for stray objects, your arms in perpetual motion, your legs never pausing during the full five minutes. Pretend you're in an aerobics class! In your apartment, the most logical order would be bathroom, bedroom, kitchen, living room—exit.

In her housekeeping book, *Totally Organized* (St. Martin's Press), Bonnie McCullough recommends the reverse order: front hall and living room first because they're most vulnerable to scrutiny by unexpected guests. That way will better fit your lifestyle someday when Mr. Wonderful, whoever he may be, plants you and our grandchildren in that darling suburban bungalow.

The hardest part of the flying five-minute pickup is forcing yourself not to stir from the room for any reason whatever until it's finished. Self-restraint is not automatic, even after forty years of housekeeping.

Having returned to your tidy apartment and fixed yourself a snack, you've done the dishes. Finished at last! Nope, not quite. While the dishcloth is still sudsy, run it over the counter and stove, and around the cupboard pulls where smudges accumulate. Take a minute more, grab a paper towel, and skim over the floor. (Buy only cheap paper towels and use them with abandon.) These quick little two-minute wipe-ups will let you get by with fewer serious cleanings. Who wants to spend all her weekends scrubbing floors? Since you work at a

desk all day, the daily bending and stretching won't hurt you a bit, either. Why, even little old ladies have been known to derive benefits from it.

A couple of waxings a year should keep your kitchen floor scuff-resistant and socially presentable. Do them when you've torn up the house anyway with spring/fall switch-arounds. Afterwards, bask in the glow of domestic self-satisfaction.

It's too bad, in a way, that the annual spring cleaning ritual has met the fate of the carpet beater and the icebox. I know vacuum cleaners are better. So are electric refrigerators. And year-round rotation of thorough cleanings from room to room is less disruptive. But there was something therapeutic about stripping an entire house down to its naked walls and floors . . . then washing the paint or erasing the year's soil off the wallpaper with balls of fragrant, gummy pink wallpaper cleaner that were fun to knead with your palms and fingers, like gobs of Play-Doh . . . whacking the daylights (plus some personal frustrations) out of the carpet on the clothesline with a wire beater, and, finally, returning every spanked, scrubbed, fresh-aired, and sun-bathed item in the house back where it belonged. No-longer-needed items went to charities or to attics to be discovered by another generation. It was a week of utter chaos followed by the sweetest imaginable calm.

But, hon, I'm glad you're part of this era of housekeeping, not that one. Who would want the return of coal stoves and furnaces belching gritty soot into the atmosphere? With so many women working outside of as well as in their homes, houses should now serve our needs and not we, theirs.

On that subject, I would heartily recommend a couple of little servants that I adore, my two dusting wands. I have a lamb's wool duster—plus a feather one with a telescoping rod for high places. Nobody has left messages in the dust on our furniture since I've had them. They make dusting simple. Just flick, flick, and a room is presentable. You could do your entire living room in the few seconds between the time the doorbell rings and when you answer the door.

Whenever the spirit moves you, do a behind-and-under-things dusting and furniture polishing at the same time. Monthly, try to move chairs, tables, etc., for a thorough cleaning. Once a year, move everything, even the heavy furniture standing against the wall. (Pretend you're Grandma, and it's spring cleaning time.) At least once a week, vacuum the main traffic path, moving up and down, then perpendicularly across the rugs or carpet. Actually, my professional carpet cleaner told me to do this every day. It's a goal, but I don't do it.

Our carpets would stay much cleaner if we weren't too boneheaded to copy some of the sensible customs of other cultures, such as slipping off our shoes at the front door. How absurd it is to persist in tracking street dirt throughout our homes on our shoes, especially ones with sponge rubber soles.

Change it, Cathy. Your generation is smarter than ours and more cordial to foreign ways.

Tedious jobs can melt away if you do them to music and concentrate on how pretty it's going to look when you're done. Home sweet home, dear.

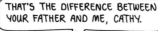

2 *Getting Organized*

Just thinking about getting organized is enough to make you sick. (Is that why in the old days ladies had so many fainting spells and took to their beds?) Getting organized is one of the least appealing, but most rewarding, aspects of running a home. The task looks formidable. It's not easy, but neither is it as hard as it looks.

Fortify yourself with all the working tools you can lay your hands on: pads, shelves, boxes, labels, notebooks, file cards—whatever you think might help, plus determination and patience.

Make a list, nip off to the store (at our house, of course, that's step one), and when you return with your sackful of supplies, start somewhere. Anywhere. A drawer, a closet, a shelf. It doesn't matter. Fifteen minutes' worth will make a difference. An hour's worth will leave you glowing with pride. Small victories are the rewards of keeping house.

Every task you complete will sparkle like a jewel among the remaining clutter. Pile after pile, you'll watch order emerge from chaos and you'll live for the day when there's nothing left to do but enjoy, enjoy, enjoy life in your lovely home. At least, that's the hope I've lived on for eons. (I suspect you have your own idea how close to succeeding I've come.)

You may already have experienced how easy it is to find yourself drowning in mail. Each day brings new waves of it. The glance-and-pitch method of disposal

is best. Unless it's a letter from a friend, a bill, something you've ordered, or information about a worthwhile cause, don't bother opening it. It's an intrusion; just pitch it. Be more sensible than your mother, Cathy; do as she says, not as she does.

Sort what you've kept into stacks of bills, letters, miscellaneous communications, and periodicals. Dad, having been trained by his secretary for many years, is especially good at this and often does it for me. (It helps to have a helper in the house.) When you've finished sorting, whip the periodicals out of sight into a magazine rack or next to your bed to be read at your leisure. Resist glancing through them now.

Instead, slit open the envelopes with your letter opener, and get through the day's mail. If you keep a supply of attractive note cards handy, you can dash off one- or two-line acknowledgments almost as quickly as you can read the contents of the letters. You'll spare yourself weeks of agonizing over delayed replies.

Any follow-up epistles can be composed some dateless Saturday night.

Keep a drawer full of file folders for information you wish to keep or refer to. It will get the papers off your desk and into retrievable order.

I hate to admit how many years it took me to realize that address books should be loose-leaf style with replaceable pages. Since I've wised up and make entries in pencil only, my address book no longer looks as though I let the grandchildren scribble in it. A miniature one for your purse comes in handy. But, as a business person, you should be telling me about dealing with addresses.

Our family calendar each year is the month-at-a-glance variety with a lot of blank writing space. Around the first of January, I go through it month by month, jotting in all birthdays, anniversaries, and special occasions that will need to be acknowledged with cards, notes, or gifts. Because it's a calendar that Dad and I refer to daily, we seldom forget important dates. Events for which we buy season tickets are noted in their appropriate spaces, as are medical and dental appointments. We pencil in tentative travel dates and ink them in as plans firm up. Invitations and special events are added as they arrive. At the end of the year, I save the calendar. It bridges us into the next year and serves as a sketchy, but accurate, diary of the previous year's events. I still have several of your old Girl Scout calendars in our storage room. Some afternoon when you're in the mood for some nostalgia, I'll dig them out for you.

Another handy convenience is a "remember to" envelope for your purse. Into it you can slip claim checks, shopping lists, and other reminders to help you consolidate your errands.

Notebooks got you through school, and they can continue to keep you on course now. Each January I fill an oversize three-ring binder with a dozen or so nine-by-twelve envelopes with cut-off tops. With a three-ring hole-punch, I perforate their sides and label each one to deal with some aspect of our personal record keeping. That includes bills to be paid, categories for various kinds of receipts, warranties and guarantees, and basic postal necessities, plus account numbers and names of people to contact. This fat notebook keeps all our bill-paying and tax reporting information in one place and is easy to work with. Some other arrangement may work better for you as long as you keep all the information and supplies together and readily available. It's harder to procrastinate when you're prepared not to.

LIFE BEFORE THE 3-RING BINDER:

LIFE AFTER THE 3-RING BINDER:

Now that your paper work's in order, let's move on to clothing. Do you realize that it takes only one step to put away a garment, but four steps not to? One, to toss it; two, to retrieve it; three, to return it where it belongs; and four, to iron it so it's fit to be seen in again. Think about it. Are you really in that big a hurry?

Leave your shoes in their original boxes except for the few you wear most often. They'll stack neatly, will be easy to find, and won't keep tumbling all over each other on the floor.

When it comes to closets, doll, I'm not the person to emulate. Except for trying to keep mine tidy and moderately organized, I'm a closet failure. Too often I catch myself putting away the winter clothes in August and the summer ones in February. The one redeeming aspect of being so out of step is that the timing is season-perfect for the charities which get the hand-me-downs. Mothers aren't perfect. They just expect their children to be.

Be sure that what you put away for next year is clean and mended. Dry cleaners will clean and repair, but not press, your garments until next season if you so request. Some will even store boxes of cleaned, out-of-season clothing for a nominal fee. With as little closet space as you have, that could be worth investigating.

Clear plastic boxes—how could I live without them? Sometimes they're even more valuable than what goes into them. Large sweater boxes hold purses, hats, sweaters, out-of-season clothing, all perfectly visible and accessible. Medium and shoe sizes are infinitely useful for desk, bathroom, bedroom, pantry, and kitchen. Into them go souvenirs, cassette tapes, unmounted snapshots, lingerie, accessories, all neatly contained but showing. In dressers, closets, and cupboards, they're the ultimate convenience. Transparent fishing tackle boxes (hardware, variety, and sporting goods stores carry them) are ideal for keeping jewelry neatly sorted, especially earrings, one pair per cubicle.

Portable stacking shelf units, both enclosed and open, saved my life the first dozen or so times we moved. We had enough of them to create instant storage walls in living, bed, and dining rooms. We piled them on top of one another and sideways as room dividers. Individually, they stood in kitchens, bathrooms, and closets, wherever needed in each new residence.

The portable units provide an easy-to-stay-organized system for transferring from one residence to another. With your surroundings changed, but your system undisturbed, you can settle right in, pretty much intact. It's awful to have to start all over again, struggling through packing boxes, each time you move. Life has not been the same since we left our shelf units in Michigan some years ago.

Ours were unpainted wood. We used them natural until we got around to painting them a neutral earth tone; they blended right in wherever we moved. Sears, K mart, and similar stores carry ample varieties.

Look them over, hon. I think you could use some.

Here's a starter list for supplies to get organized:
- Stackable shelf units, wood if possible
- Clear plastic storage boxes (prefer clear plastic lids) in three sizes: shoe, lingerie, sweater

- Clear plastic fishing tackle boxes (for jewelry)
- One- or two-drawer small filing cabinet . . . or box to fit file folders
- File folders
- Gummed labels
- 3-ring notebook, extra-large size
- 9- by 12-inch envelopes (to use in notebook)
- 3-hole paper punch (single hole-punch okay)
- Ruler, prefer 18-inch
- Assortment of office supplies (scissors, marking pens, note pads, etc.)

Getting organized has another aspect that might be worth mentioning. It's dressing for an engagement.

When you have to catch a train, bus, or plane, you make it with time to spare, right? But when a friend is waiting in your living room, the same brain that got you to the plane on time starts dragging you through a series of indecisions about what to put on. Half a closetful of deliberations may come to rest on your bed before you actually leave the house frazzled, rather than calmly collected, as you had envisioned. Poor Dad; all those years of it with me!

But no longer. Not since I've taken to heart some advice from my friend Helen Griffith, a newspaper columnist who earns a living attending social functions punctually and appropriately dressed. I've tried Helen's way and it works. Here's how:

Early in the day (not after racing home from the office late and hassled), lay out exactly what you will wear that evening. No changes of mind permitted once the decision is made! Lay out every bit, including underwear, stockings, jewelry, and a handbag filled with everything you'll need. If there's something to bring, hang it on the doorknob or attach a reminder to the door.

Not only does this permit you to ascertain in advance that what you plan to wear hasn't a spot or wrinkle or snag (giving you time to rectify it or change course), but it also enables you to dress in minutes instead of hours.

And just think, sweetie pie, should you feel a hospitable urge to invite your friend in afterwards, your apartment will be ready and waiting—not strewn with hair curlers, ironing board, sewing kit, and a pile of clothes you decided against.

How about that for a change?

3   *Kitchens*

Kitchens remind me of children. If you don't keep after them, they can turn into monsters. But if you pay attention to them, devoting time to make friends with them, they'll give you much pleasure with very little trouble. You need to wipe them off daily, scrub as needed, and replenish regularly with food and beverage. No problem. They're filled with creative potential . . . so they're worth it.

Of course, if you don't use the kitchen except to make coffee or get a drink of water, it won't give you any trouble at all. (Even then you must wash the dishes from time to time because it's unsanitary not to, and, besides, there's no one else to do it for you.)

The smaller the kitchen, the harder it is to keep tidy. You're not messy, sweetie; your kitchen's just too small. However, for the amount of cooking you do, it's kitchen enough for you. No matter what its size, you should keep things handy so that even with your eyes shut you can reach instantly for whatever you need. Later you must return it to that very same place. "A place for everything and everything in its place" is crucial in the kitchen. Otherwise, cooking can be a monstrous chore.

The need for orderliness extends even to the food in your cupboard. Unless you subsist on commercially frozen dinners, you'll find it impossible to put together a meal without a supply of basic staples. The way *you* use them, though, it will be years before you use up such things as flour, sugar, grains, and spices. So, wrap them securely in plastic to keep them fresh as long as possible. (The world's neatest kitchens are loaded with plastic . . . plastic bags, plastic containers, plastic wrap, plastic food . . . of course not, silly. I just wanted to see if you were still paying attention. Now that the microwave oven has become king of the kitchen, you can even cook in plastic.)

Let me take a minute to warn you about organic staples. They are full of little critters that can nibble through their containers and hatch all over your house as moths. Even mighty plastic can't confine them once they're ready to emerge. Be sure to sift the flour and rinse the grains before using unprocessed products.

What you cook in has a lot to do with the success or failure of your effort. You'd be better off, for instance, with one or two sturdy, well-constructed cooking pots than a cupboard full of thin, poor quality ones in which everything except water will scorch. One good pan (I happen to be partial to stainless steel) and one good skillet (Grandma's favorite cast-iron still is unsurpassed) should be priority investments.

On second thought, a simple step-by-step cookbook should be first, then the pots.

Finding a good elementary cookbook should be no problem. Two that I'd not hesitate to recommend are Craig Claiborne's *Kitchen Primer* (Vintage Books division of Random House) and *Sunset Easy Basics for Good Cooking* by the editors of *Sunset* magazine (Lane Publishing Co.). Both are paperbacks.

But back to your cookware.

Unlike today's "light" foods and beverages, heavy is better when it comes to pots and pans. Burnt food is what you'll get out of thin ones whose bottoms buckle on contact with heat. A non-stick surface is especially desirable for skillets. Trusty old cast-iron pots cook food evenly; they won't undermine your confidence with burnt offerings. Like friendship, cast-iron requires some cultivating. It needs to be seasoned with use and will rust if neglected.

Many homemakers prefer skillets of heavy nonstick aluminum; they do an excellent job. But much as I like stainless steel, I have yet to find a frying pan made of it that I feel I can trust. They overheat too quickly and cool off too slowly. They may be the handsomest of the whole culinary lot, but that doesn't make them the best prospects for your kitchen . . . if I may offer a motherly analogy.

Would it help if you had a guide list of kitchen equipment? If so, here's one. The sizes suggested are approximate. In case the sauce pans or skillets you buy don't come with lids, get clear Pyrex ones. It's nice to see what's going on under the lid.

For starters:
- Cookbook
- 2-quart saucepan
- 10-inch skillet
- 9- by 13-inch baking pan
- 9-inch Pyrex cake pan
- 2-quart casserole
- 10-inch chef's knife
- Wooden spoon
- Manual can opener
- Bottle opener
- Electric hand mixer

- 4-inch paring knife
- Vegetable peeler
- Nested mixing bowls
- Nested measuring cups
- Measuring spoons
- Rubber spatula
- Slotted turner
- Chopping board
- Toaster
- Small stainless strainer

After your first raise:
- 1-quart saucepan
- 4-quart saucepan or pot
- Wire whisk
- Manual grater/shredder
- Flour sifter
- Rolling pin

- Garlic press
- Funnel
- Large stainless strainer
- Colander
- Corkscrew

After your next raise:
- 8-quart pot
- Omelet pan
- Heavy-duty electric mixer
- Electric blender
- Electric can opener
- More sturdy knives
- Salad spinner
  (for drying lettuce, etc.)

- Microwave oven
- Microwave cookware
- Timer
- Ladle
- Spatula
- Whatever else your
  kitchen wants that your
  pocketbook can afford

One final thought: Before you sit down to eat, fill the cooking utensils with hot soapy water. They'll soak themselves practically clean while you eat. If you hand wash and put away preparation tools as you use them, you won't return from the dining table to a mess in the kitchen. An unkempt kitchen is no fun. Besides, what if someone should drop in?

Good grief, I nearly forgot! You'll need a wall-mounted erasable board (a child's chalkboard works well). I'd forget my head without mine. No wall space? A note pad will do but they, like children, never seem to be where you want them when you need them.

4 *Marketing*

Marketing is one of the chores you found so boring that you seldom would accompany me to do it. Now that there's no escaping it, don't you wish you had come along more often and paid more attention?

Really, though, you weren't that different from other mothers' daughters. Neither was I. Still, we try to spare our children needless hard lumps. If only we could make our darlings less like we were! Thank goodness they turn out better than we do anyway. In spite of all our blunders we parents are rewarded with young adults who surpass our expectations. That makes ours the best paid job in the world. No amount of money could ever bring the satisfaction of a child grown into a beautiful, responsible adult.

Enough can't be said in praise of the young parents of today—mothers who hold down full-time jobs while they raise families—often with limited help from their husbands—or those young fathers who have broken out of the stereotyped molds to share the domestic duties. How in the world do any of them manage to fit the weekly marketing into schedules like theirs?

Now that you're responsible for buying your own supplies, sweetie, how about making it easier on yourself? It's perfectly permissible, you know, to have an extra roll of toilet paper and a spare can of coffee in the house. You don't have to live from crisis to crisis. Think about it *before* the cupboard registers empty.

It may not be spellbinding reading, but force yourself to scan the weekly grocery ads and circulars. Soon you'll have some comprehension of what different items should cost and will recognize a bargain when you see one. You'll also realize which items are overpriced and you can buy them later on sale or at another store.

Back when you were a schoolgirl and coupons first started appearing in grocery store ads, I would deliberately avoid that store and make my purchases elsewhere. Doing business at a store that sells to everyone at a reasonable price felt better. It still does. Why should a store charge two different customers different prices for the same item purchased at the same time?

Fine-tooth combing the newspaper for coupons, clipping them, tracking down the items in the stores, making sure the necessary coupons are in your purse at the check-out . . . what a waste of time and effort! There are people with the time and inclination for couponing who have made hobbies or mini-careers

of it. More power to them while the opportunity exists. In self-defense I use my share.

But the coupon craze seems especially unfair to young working people like you who simply haven't the time to take advantage of it. Because of coupons, groceries probably cost you more than they do the coupon packin' mama next door. Actually your couponing time might be better spent improving your career skills.

Cashiers appreciate it when you hand them your coupons before they've rung everything up. Any store which sells the merchandise is obliged to honor the coupons but, obviously, it's a bigger nuisance to the mom-and-popper than to the supermarket.

Reduced prices with no coupons or rebates would suit me just fine. Sales, I like! They create no-holds-barred opportunities to save and are a 100 percent fair-to-everyone option; in fact, they're fun! Toilet paper and cleaning supplies, especially, are nice to load up on whenever you can find your preferred brands (stick with them!) on sale.

When you walk the aisles with a list in hand, you'll succumb to fewer tempting displays of items that you can get along without just fine.

Find a recipe you'd like to try, and make a grocery list. Even if you absentmindedly leave it at home, as I'm likely to, your brain will remember most of what you wrote. Because it's time-consuming, you should stick to weekend marketing until you're familiar enough with the routine to whip through it easily after work. Eventually you will have repeated the same steps so often that gathering necessities will scarcely faze you.

Thanks to modern labeling, meats, poultry, and produce are easily identifiable in their clear plastic (here we go again!) wrappings. What a help to be able to glance at a package and know the name and weight and price of what you're looking at.

My first encounter as a young bride with the neighborhood grocer could have devastated my new marriage. What I saw at the store bore no resemblance to meals I had been served at home or in restaurants. I had no idea what to ask for by name or how much of it might weigh a pound or how much would yield one serving. Your sweet, patient father and I ate eggs and hot dogs until I regained the courage to try again. Both Dad and I survived, so did the marriage, and so will you.

It's difficult for a single person to buy food in small enough quantities that she doesn't wind up overeating or throwing away spoiled food. With starving people in the world, the money wasted would better have been given to some mission. Or you could even have saved it for your old age.

Resist ready-mixed "meal helper" concoctions. They run up your bill without providing much nourishment. I try never to be without a package of instant rice which I seldom use. It's a marvelous time-saver for emergencies, but it's no nutritional bargain. Brown rice is infinitely better. It tastes better and is better for you. Cook rice in bouillon-flavored water with a dab of butter plus an optional piece of garlic. Start it an hour before you plan to eat. What a feast!

It's wise to carry your checkbook—just in case! Groceries always gobble up dollars faster than you'd suspect when you're accumulating them in the cart.

If you'd like a rough idea of the kinds of grocery items I've found especially helpful, here's a list:

Housekeeping Survival List

Never-run-out-of's:
- Toilet paper
- Toilet soap
- Paper towels
- Facial tissues
- A friendly neighbor, at least one

Multipurpose cleaners:
- Vinegar
- Baking soda
- Ammonia
- Spray and wipe liquids
- All-purpose liquid or powder
- A willing mother

Kitchen sinkers:
- Dishwashing detergent
- Scouring cleanser (non-bleach is milder)
- Scouring pads
- Nontarnish cleaners for silver, copper, brass
- Sponges
- Rubber gloves
- A willing boyfriend

Bathroom maintainers:
- Toilet bowl cleaner with disposable pads
- Glass cleaner spray
- Sponges
- Rubber gloves
- Paper towels
- Liquid scrub or powdered nonchlorine cleanser
- All-purpose cleaning liquid

Grooming economizers:
- Gallon-size shampoo (name brand)
- Gallon-size hair conditioner (name brand)
- Hydrogen peroxide solution for mouth rinse (dilute with water)

- Baking soda
- Pantry products for hair, face, and body

Laundry dirt chasers:
- All-purpose detergent, liquid preferred
- Detergent for delicates, liquid or powder
- Powder bluing, to brighten whites and "lights"
- Water softener (if in hard-water area)
- Cake of naphtha soap ('cause Grandma used it)
- Prewash spray for spots, etc.
- Grease-removing liquid
- Fabric softener (optional)
- A hired laundress

Handy spot removers:
- Club soda
- Hair spray
- Bleach
- Vinegar
- Hydrogen peroxide solution
- Special commercial products
- Baking soda
- Lemon
- Sunshine
- Your friendly neighborhood professional dry cleaner

General housekeepers:
- Dusting wand, either lamb's wool or feather
- Rags and sponges
- Furniture soap
- Furniture polish
- Wax, paste and liquid
- Spray guard (to protect upholstery)
- Vacuum cleaner, standard size
- Hand-held vacuum
- A weekly maid (or willing mother)

Pantry standbys:
- Flour, all-purpose unbleached—2-pound bag
- Sugar, salt, pepper, etc.
- Cornstarch or arrowroot powder (thickeners)

- Rice—long-cooking brown (yum!)
- Instant rice (for emergencies)
- Noodles, spaghetti, etc.
- Assortment of basic spices and herbs (cinnamon, nutmeg, etc.)
- Brown sugar (dark)
- Vinegar (suit yourself on type)
- Cooking/salad oil (olive or sunflower seed)
- Mustard (imported Dijon is best)
- Ketchup
- Mayonnaise
- Soy sauce
- Coffee
- Tea (herbal—bags more convenient)
- Bottled lemon juice
- Garlic, fresh (powder tastes awful)
- Onion, fresh whole plus jar of flaked
- Tomato sauce, jar or can
- Mushrooms, jar or can
- Can of mushroom soup (for casseroles)
- Can of tomato soup (just because)
- Milled or miller's bran (nature's own laxative)
- Telephone line to Mom
- Pickles

- Olives
- Dried grated cheese
- Fat pocketbook

Quickie meal-fixers:

- Frozen dinners
- Frozen vegetables, large size bags (use portions as needed)
- Frozen juice concentrate
- Dehydrated soup mixes
- Canned soups
- Spaghetti sauce, jar or can
- Canned tuna, chicken, salmon, etc.

Company dazzlers:

- Frozen cooked shrimp
- Can of hearts of palm
- Can of artichoke hearts
- Tin of lobster or crabmeat
- Package of cream cheese (for spreads, dips)
- Cans of cream-style soups
- Jar or can of mushrooms
- Instant rice
- Gourmet crackers
- Tin of anchovies
- Gobs of imagination

5   *Cooking*

Well, it had to happen sometime, Cathy.

Here goes a closely guarded domestic trade secret: If you can read a fourth-grade book, you can cook. No fooling! Cooking is nowhere near as complicated or mysterious as the Great Mom Brigade has let on. Anyone can do it who is willing to put together food and utensils and subject them to heat or to cold. All you have to do is line up your ingredients and, step by step, simply follow the instructions. That's it. Voilà, you're a cook!

If you keep an assortment of fresh fruits and vegetables on hand, you'll seldom need to cook because most of them are better for you raw. Vegetables cook in a very few minutes (sliced carrots, three; asparagus, five; broccoli, eight to ten, my top of the head guess). They should feel crisp, not limp, when bitten. You'll miss it the first few times, but don't worry. Dad has downed plenty of my mistakes. You'll do better next time.

Vitamin retention is best when you use the least amount of water your heavy-bottom pot will tolerate (a couple of tablespoons or so) without scorching. Cover, cook on high heat until lid jiggles, immediately reduce heat to low. No peeking until you suspect it's done. This method steams them in their own juice.

For company meals, you want to do it the French way. The results are spectacular. Bring an ample potful of water to a rolling boil (yes, salt it a little), drop in vegetables, bring back to brisk boil, and let them bounce merrily uncovered on high heat for one to five minutes. Grab out a piece from minute to minute to test for doneness. Drain immediately in very cold water. Drain again and hold until almost serving time. The colors stay brilliant and the textures crisp. To serve, reheat quickly at the very last minute. It's delicious and impressive, but you do rinse some vitamins down the drain. Be sure to use bigger pots to cook vegetables this way; they can't be crowded.

Eat a nice fresh salad every day, either fruit or vegetable. If you didn't have one for lunch and don't have the fixings in the refrigerator, stop on the way home at a fast-food restaurant with a salad bar. The variety of fresh ingredients would be hard to duplicate at home for the same price, when you consider that it takes time to shop for and prepare the vegetables and trimmings. Later, in the evening you can have a piece of fruit or some cheese. You'll be well-nourished and won't spend the evening snacking on doughnuts or cookies which shouldn't have sneaked into your grocery bag in the first place.

Any conglomeration of leftover vegetables, cooked or raw, can be dropped into the blender. Add some liquid—bouillon, vegetable juice, yogurt, whatever your imagination inspires—plus some seasoning and whir up a thick, nutritious soup. What a delicious, satisfying meal you can have in minutes, with practically no mess . . . Run some hot tap water into the blender, add a drop of dish detergent, turn it on, and it will blend itself clean in seconds. Rinse, drain, and your work is done. No stacks of pots and pans. Just a single bowl and spoon that you can dispose of with a hot soapy sponge.

Save a week's worth of leftovers in plastic for a tasty soup or casserole. If you're not certain you'll use them within two days, freeze the dabs. They'll come in handy when you want to put something together in a hurry without a trip to the grocery. Keep a couple of cans of mushroom, tomato, cheese, or other soup in the cupboard to help convert your dabs into a creation. Grease a casserole dish, then dump the soup from the can on to the dabs and heat. It tastes bland? Add some imaginative seasoning. Bouillon, lemon juice, yogurt, mayonnaise, fruit juices, mustard, spices, or anything else that pops into your head is worth a try. Don't be inhibited. You'll have more successes than failures, and much more fun.

You know, don't you, that dairy products can be frozen. I keep an extra pound of butter in the freezer—and pop in the cheese, milk, and cream when we go on trips. It's nice to have something on hand when we return. Refrigerated fresh eggs are usable for up to a month.

It's thrifty not to throw out—but bad to throw together—warmed or room temperature foods with refrigerated ones. That means, sweetie, don't pour the milk or cream from the pitcher back into the bottle after dinner. Keep the used portion separate for reuse. Otherwise the whole batch can spoil sooner. This is especially true of dairy products, but cooked leftovers should be treated the same way. For instance, if you reheat a portion of yesterday's stew, either pitch what you couldn't finish tonight or store it in a separate container. The healthiest way is thriftiest of all.

Fresh fish and boned pieces of chicken cook quickly. Start them in the skillet and ten to twenty minutes later, depending on their thickness, you can be eating. Touch test a piece with your finger or poke it with a fork. If it yields and bounces right back, it's done. Hamburger or steak can be done even quicker depending on how pink inside you like it. Roasts are for weekends. They're easiest of all but can't be hurried.

Baking you should bag. It takes too much time and it piles up on you as f-a-t. Who has the strength to resist stuffing herself with warm, fresh out-of-the-oven goodies? Better to stop at the bakery and treat yourself to a couple of pieces rather than tempt yourself with a whole batch. Even the surprises you bake for friends will sneak up on you. (The bakery's probably will taste better anyway.) But unless you pop them into the freezer to preserve their freshness, baked goods will be unappetizing the day after you buy them. Eat what you want, then freeze the rest.

Getting several things to finish cooking at the same time is not easy. There's no painless way to learn meal timing. So, when the first thing is ready, just enjoy it as a separate course. The only way to master timing is practice. In a few years it'll be perfect.

And, Cathy, unless you're making a career or hobby of cooking, keep it

simple. Save your craving for the fancy gourmet stuff for when you eat out. Let someone else slave for hours to produce a work of culinary art. Plain-but-nutritious is plenty good at home.

For home or family consumption, milk makes fine sauces, even when cream is called for. But if the boss and his wife or other equally important guests are coming, use whipping cream. Your sauce will turn out perfect. It won't separate or curdle or otherwise embarrass you. The result is worth a calorie or two.

If you get stuck midway through a recipe, remember that it makes a mother's heart fairly flutter with delight to have a daughter ask for advice (do you hear mine thumping?). Or, phone a friend who's more experienced than you. In short order you, too, will be a cook—or as much of one as you want to be. It's no reflection on womanhood not to be particularly good at it or to do it at all, for that matter. Cooking can be an optional skill.

Even today it's possible to eat rather well at a modest cost. Dried beans, peas, lentils, rice, and barley can help make nourishing, tasty soups. Use bony chicken parts or beef bones or ham bones or bouillon powder to flavor the broth. Add salt, pepper, paprika, celery, carrots, parsley, onion, garlic, potato, or whatever other vegetable is in the refrigerator. It's a good way to get extra meals out of less desirable portions of meat. If you're having someone over for T-bones, for instance, trim the meat off the bone before you cook it, and put the bones in the freezer to use for soup another time. The same with chicken.

Some of the most delicious meals at our home were made by Grandma from throwaway parts that you find on few modern tables: tripe, kidneys, hearts, neckbones, oxtails, tongue, and sweetbreads, to mention a few.

Cabbage and potatoes helped our family survive the Depression. Grandma flavored the cabbage with a bacon roux. Though we ate it almost daily for about three years, I'd welcome a plate of it tomorrow—without any Depression, of course.

Whether you're fighting a cold or are just plain hungry, it's comforting to know there's a pot of soup in the kitchen. The fragrance permeating the air as it simmers on the burner has greater allure than any perfume counter. And economical—why you could live all next week on Saturday's potful! The recipe is so simple it's virtually fail-proof. Let me give you a lesson on soup that I learned from my mother, and never again suffer any qualms cooking it homemade.

A basic soup is nothing but a generous potful of heated water plus seasonings, vegetables, and, usually, some bony meat or fowl. Though the meat, fowl and bone are not mandatory, they add flavor and nutrients. In the fowl to water ratio, the less water, the richer the end product will be. For instance, if you cook a three-pound chicken in three quarts of water, the broth will be richer and tastier than if you had immersed the same chicken in five quarts of water. After the broth firms up in the refrigerator, scrape any solidified fat off the top. If it firms up as thick as jellied consomme, you may want to add a bit of water to the portion you remove to reheat. Or, if it turns out thinner or blander than it should have, perk it up with powdered bouillon (I'm not partial to the cubes; too salty). Reheat soup one serving at a time, and the balance of it will stay good for a week, refrigerated (chicken might be questionable after five days).

Beef soup can be made of soup bone alone (about two pounds; if it's a large knuckle bone, have the butcher chop it in half to release more of the gelatinous inner material during cooking) or any kind of beef, such as chuck or short ribs plus some extra bone, or just the meat plus some bouillon. Cooks learn to make do with whatever they can get their hands on and compensate for what's missing.

Step number one is to rinse the meat or fowl, then drop it into a pot of cold water. Heat the water and the meat together on high just to the boiling point, then immediately reduce the heat to simmer on low for the remainder of the cooking period. (The reason you want to avoid a rolling boil is that it results in a cloudy instead of a clear broth.) Some scummy-looking material will foam up on the surface. Skim it off with a strainer. Do this several times during the next fifteen to twenty minutes until the surface looks clear. At this point, add the seasonings. This is step two. Include garlic, onions, and parsley during step two. After an hour of step two, proceed with step three: adding the vegetables. Cook for about an hour longer. Remove meat or chicken when it's obviously done. The broth can simmer a while longer if it needs to develop more flavor.

Taste it from time to time, adjusting the seasonings until it tastes right. In case you have over-salted it, drop in a couple of peeled raw potatoes. They'll absorb the excess.

The base of meatless soups can be vegetable bouillon or a roux of flour and butter cooked to a light brown paste before water is added. A roux is made by melting a couple of tablespoons of butter or bacon drippings or other shortening, blending flour into it; add liquid, some salt, and any other seasonings you wish. To make creamed soups (as well as creamed eggs, chicken à la king, macaroni and cheese, etc.), add the milk before the flour begins to brown.

When cooking dried beans, peas, lentils, barley, etc., add them to the water during step two along with the seasonings. While the dried legumes cook, prepare any fresh vegetables, chopping them bite-size, to add during the last half hour or so of cooking.

Now that you understand homemade soup, here's a basic recipe to play with when you have time.

Soup

- 3 to 3^1/$_2$-pound chicken (or beef and bone)
- 3^1/$_2$ quarts water
- 2 tablespoons salt (more or less to suit your taste)
- 1 teaspoon pepper
- 1 teaspoon paprika

- 2 or 3 cloves garlic
- 1 onion
- 1 tablespoon parsley flakes (or handful of fresh)
- 2 to 4 carrots, depending on size
- 4 stalks celery (or their equivalent in leafy tops)

Simmer partially covered for 2 to 3 hours.

In a separate pot, cook some noodles, rice, or spaetzle dumplings. Place in individual bowls, and ladle soup over them. Add meat or chicken if you wish, but usually it's served as a separate course.

6 *Entertaining*

One of the nicest bonuses of having a nest of your own is the freedom it gives you to invite whomever you wish, whenever you wish. If you think small and build your confidence gradually, in no time at all you'll feel the urge to hostess something more daring.

To get started, invite a co-worker to stop by after work for deli pizza and salad. Ask a neighbor in for dessert and coffee. Sunday brunch is a natural next step. Keep the menu simple; let the bakery help. By broadening your circle of acquaintances, you may uncover a friend. Seeds must be planted before they can grow.

As you become more sure of yourself, prepare one simple menu until repeated success with it inspires you to try variations and move on to another.

Even failures can germinate successful friendships. Dad and I might have missed a beaut had not "Aunt" Lou and "Uncle" George invited a couple of strangers in town (us) for blueberry waffles (their first). That the waffles had to be scraped off the iron only created more reason to get together for subsequent attempts. It wasn't long before blueberry waffles became Aunt Lou's pièce de résistance and her company meal for the next year or so. Everyone she and Uncle George knew looked forward to being invited.

Cooking for company is infinitely more inspiring than doing it just for yourself. It adds an element of excitement to otherwise prosaic tasks. If you're going to do all or most of the cooking, give yourself plenty of time. Schedule everything that needs to be done. Write it down day by day until *the* day, then hour by hour. A three-day plan is not a bad idea. You'll be sure everything is bought, cleaned, jellied, blended, baked, and ready to serve on time—and will be calmly in control to enjoy your food and your guests. Don't neglect to plan some talk topics and activity.

For a party of eight or more, it's ideal to set your table days ahead, every polished thing in place except the fresh centerpiece. Carefully spread a clean sheet or towels over it until party day. This will free your time to do something toward the party each day and reduce the risk of last-minute calamities. Having done your homework, sweetie, you can relax; the "test" will be a snap.

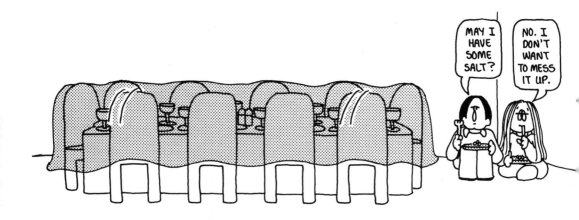

Oh, and don't forget the music. It takes music and flowers to set the mood for a party. Be as lavish with the flowers as your budget will permit.

Having a theme or special reason for a gathering creates a focal point for both decoration and menu. It opens the door to conversations between strangers. It also makes it easier for the hostess to stay in charge throughout the evening with games and questions that encourage everyone's participation. But if you can't think of a good excuse, for goodness sake, don't wait. Go ahead and set the date. Wanting to entertain is excuse enough.

My most inspired house cleanings have happened as a result of having planned a party. Long-neglected tasks practically did themselves in joyous

anticipation. Actually, the cleaning is more optional than necessary. When time is short, here's what seasoned housewives do: Forget any fancy cleaning! Just flick a cloth or feather duster over the most obvious places, polish the entry, and prepare a sparkling bathroom, including insides of cabinets (just in case), adding fresh flowers and towels (the ones you've set aside for guest appearances only). Next, put the kitchen in order before anyone shows up because that's where guests gravitate. Skip the vacuuming. They'll never notice, and you'll have to do it afterwards anyway. Set the timer to monitor what's cooking, light the candles, and enjoy your lovely dinner and your friends.

While you're at it, you may as well have another group the following night. The house is ready. The flowers will still be fresh. And if you present the dinner attractively, who, except you, will know that leftovers are being served?

Before the restaurant Sunday brunch became mecca for church-going (and laggard) Americans, the Sunday dinner at home was a tradition. Except for weddings, christenings, holidays, and after-the-funeral farewells, Sunday was pretty much *it* when it came to hostessing.

Grandma would work all Saturday baking and preparing the feast for whomever she and Grandpa decided to invite on the way out of church the next morning. With not much else going on, this was not considered "last minute" in those days. Place settings were roughed in until an accurate head count could be made. It also gave Grandma a reason to let guests help finish setting the table while she finished getting the dinner (you "got" dinner in those days). When guests lingered into the evening, the noon meal's leftovers were served, usually cold. It was informal and relaxed—a comfortable mixture of family and friends, with the children always present.

Unless you're entertaining formally or elegantly, letting a guest help is an easy icebreaker. "Help" can be something as simple as filling the water glasses. Aunt Mabel's standard welcome to new people at church was to whisper on the way out, "Come have dinner with us, but please run the sweeper while Harold mashes the potatoes and I make the gravy." Who could resist such an invitation to friendship? "Aunt" Mabel and "Pappy" (Harold) adopted whole families, including ours. They had a gift for making people feel needed and wanted and special.

Today our ways of entertaining may have changed, but the key to doing it graciously has not. Love having your guests! They'll know it when you do. Setting a little something or other before a drop-in friend is a pleasant expression of hospitality. You'll be amazed at how little you need to have on hand to whip up an impromptu snack.

For instance:

If you have . . .
> some assorted cold meat,
>
> cheese,
>
> mustard,
>
> pickles or olives,
>
>> you can serve hot or cold sandwiches, either closed or open-face.

If you have . . .
> cream cheese,
>
> chopped nuts,
>
> chopped green olives,
>
> a tablespoon or so of cream,
>
>> you can serve a tasty dip or spread or sandwich.

If you have . . .
> an English muffin,
>
> a slice of tomato or some tomato-based sauce,
>
> any dabs of vegetable, meat, or fish (optional),
>
> some cheese,
>
>> you can serve a mini pizza.

If you have . . .
> a can of tuna, salmon, or chicken,
>
> ¼ of an onion or more,
>
> mayonnaise,
>
> a tomato or avocado,
>
>> you can serve a fish or chicken salad in a "boat."

If you have . . .

    a can of cream style corn,

    ¼ cup of cream or milk,

        you can serve a bowl of cream of corn soup.

If you have . . .

    2 hard-boiled eggs or a jar of dried beef,

    1 tablespoon of butter,

    1 tablespoon of flour,

    ½ cup of milk,

    some toast,

        you can serve creamed eggs or beef on toast.

If you have . . .

    a frozen pie crust,

    3 eggs,

    1½ cups of light cream or milk,

    about 5 slices of bacon or some ham,

    about 4 slices of cheese (especially if it's Swiss),

        you can serve a classic French quiche.

If you have . . .

    a frozen pie crust,

    3 eggs,

    1½ cups of light cream or milk,

    a small package of frozen vegetables,

        you can serve a modified American quiche.

If you have . . .

    2 eggs,

    a generous teaspoon of butter,

        you can serve a delicious omelet, plain or embellished with anything you might have on hand, such as cheese, onions, leftover vegetables, etc.

If you have . . .

    2 eggs,

    ½ cup flour,

    ½ cup milk,

    ½ stick butter,

        you can serve a spectacular baked pancake (15 minutes baking time).

See? Nothing to it! Have fun, sweetie.

Grandma used to advise, "Never let the sun set on a quarrel." To which I add: or a party mess. Clean up promptly (by evening of the following day) and you'll feel like entertaining again soon.

When you do the entertaining, it's one thing, but when you have been entertained, that's another. A whole family of gentlemanly traditions, such as opening doors for ladies, helping them with their coats or chairs, appears to be gasping its last. Pleasant as such customs were, it's understandable how they might be construed as condescending or superfluous in a world of equal rights and privileges.

But another custom of extinct or presently expiring generations, like mine, hardly seems to deserve such a fate. It is the ritual of the bread-and-butter note— a genteel, if fragrant of moth balls, follow-up to the provider by the receiver of a gift or hospitality or some thoughtful service.

Believe me, hon, it's refreshing in today's bursting-with-busyness society to encounter the rare individual, such as you, who bucks the contemporary norm with a prompt thank-you note or phone call.

(The pleasure of selecting a gift or doing something special for someone lies in the anticipation of the pleasure it will give the recipient. But nowadays, how is one to know? It's awkward to have to ask, "Did you receive the gift I sent six months ago?" Of late, the sole way many a sender can be sure a gift has reached its intended recipient is to mail a check, and learn from next month's bank statement whether or not it was cashed.)

To most antiques, yours truly included, a penned thank-you note is as natural an epilogue to a dinner party, for instance, as the invitation was its prologue. It needn't be long or flowery but it must be prompt and sincere—written immediately, or even phoned the next day, before the flush of enthusiasm fades. A one- or two-liner can do it; such as:

> Dear So and So,
>   What a pleasant evening. Thanks a bunch for including me!

or:

> Dear So and So,
>   How could you know that (name of item) was exactly what I wanted. I'll think of you whenever I use it.

Even though I haven't a smidgen of doubt that it is, indeed, more blessed to give than to receive, I am convinced that the dutiful follow-up bread-and-butter note or phone call would be equally good for the soul of the receiver. Do you suppose that renaming them "soul" notes or "soul" calls would make the idea more palatable?

7   Laundry

Doing the laundry is like having a headache. It feels good to get it over with. If you had a rich husband, of course, you could have a laundress do it for you. But you would be more likely to marry somebody poor but wonderful as I did, a just-home-from-the-war soldier, and wind up with twice as much laundry and no time for a fascinating career. So, the best thing is to just face up to it and learn how to make the experience as painless as possible.

Putting it off is harder than just plunging in and getting it out of the way. Anyhow, the washing machine will do most of the work. All you have to do is sort, spot, and drop the dirty stuff into it. I get good results by filling the machine part way, pouring in the required amount of liquid detergent, and then dropping in the soiled clothes. Sometimes I add some bleach, borax, or bluing to the water before depositing the clothes. You know, don't you, that white, light-colored, and dark things are washed in separate batches? Also, that small loads wash cleaner than big ones; and that the lighter the dryer load, the fewer the wrinkles? Don't stuff the machines full!

First, rub spots with laundry soap or hair spray (it removes ball-point pen marks) or a prewash product. Some, like fruit stains, come out best if you hold them under hot running water. Others, such as blood, chocolate, and bananas should soak in cold water, then be rubbed with soap. For more stubborn stains you might try bleach, vinegar, lemon juice, peroxide, sunshine, or the working person's best friend: the professional dry cleaner. Always attack a stain immediately if possible. Blotting with club soda right away can eliminate the stain and will leave no ring.

You already know, I'm sure, that not everything should go into the washing machine. As I caution you about this, I must confess that lazy me washes silks, with a few exceptions, in the washing machine on "delicate" and hosiery in a mesh bag in the regular dark load. But to get on with the hand washing: unless wool is marked machine washable don't drop it into the washer! If you do, only the neighbor's toy poodle will be able to wear it afterwards.

If you wash, not dry clean, your favorite sweater, use only the mildest powder or liquid cleaning product. Gently squeeze out as much of the rinse water as you can *without twisting,* and roll the sweater in a clean bath towel or two to soak up the excess water. Carefully hand-stretch to the right shape and size on a towel on the floor. Do the same with any other "hand-wash-only" which could stretch out of shape if hung up to dry. Use the dry-flat-on-the-floor method, too, for

machine-washed cotton knits whose size and shape it's important to preserve.

Drip-dry clothes launder perfectly without a trace of wrinkles if lifted absolutely dripping out of the cold rinse water and hung to drip themselves completely dry, which usually is surprisingly quick. I love them!

Don't even consider laundering anything that could have its quality damaged by dunking. Have it dry cleaned. Many fabrics such as corduroy, for instance, wash beautifully but retain their new look longer if dry cleaned. As many different outfits as dressing for a career demands, you should get acquainted with your neighborhood bulk cleaners. The cost is modest compared to full service.

After the bulk cleaning attendants have weighed your bundle, they inspect and prespot each item. Once cleaned, the garments are steamed to smooth away wrinkles. In a couple of hours your things are ready to be picked up, neatly hung, folded, and plastic-wrapped. While not a deluxe full service, it's both a time and cash saver in today's busy life.

Did I ever tell you about Grandma's handy little invention for laundering delicates? She used a bucket and short-handled plunger (a plumber's helper like Dad uses the unblock the toilet) to activate sudsy water through clothing without injuring the fragile fabric. Grandmas are ingenious people. If they ran the world there would be no unsolved problems. A grandmother can find a solution to anything!

Drying your clothes requires its own little bag of tricks: Stick to low temperatures and remove most items before they're completely dry. Lift them out mid-cycle, hang to finish air-drying and you'll hardly ever need to iron them.

Then finish drying the towels and heavier things at higher temperatures. Don't give me that look (I can see it even when I can't see you). I know you would rather bone-dry everything fast on highest heat and jam it, all wadded up, into a laundry basket. But believe an experienced little old housewife, that method only shrinks, wrinkles, and creates extra work you don't need. If there's one thing we all can do without, it's work we don't need.

Speaking of which, when you and your sisters were growing up and we had overnight guests by the houseful, mountains of bedding and towels could keep our washing machine humming for days at a time. My liberation came the day I loaded everything into the car and drove to the laundromat. After distributing my mini mountain into ten washing machines and depositing the necessary coins, I sat down to enjoy a book until the "done" lights flashed on one after another of the machines.

So, Cathy, don't let any aspect of keeping house get to you. Simple solutions to all sorts of problems present themselves when you least expect them.

8   *Appearance*

Appearance is how you look and dress. It's how you feel. It's how you behave. It's how the world, in turn, appraises and responds to you. There's more to it than meets the eye.

It starts with a daily scrubbing and polishing that extends to the tips of your shoes and includes covering your body with immaculate, attractive clothing.

The clothing is never a size too small, nor does it call attention to itself in bizarre or revealing ways. Outlandish attire is normal for people in the entertainment world and is expected by adoring fans. Looking at it, not wearing it, is normal for the rest of us. Some fashion magazines can't seem to tell the difference.

Well-groomed young ladies are not seen in split seams or sagging hems. So before you put it on, make sure a button hasn't popped or a snag erupted since you last wore it. A two-minute rendezvous with needle and thread right now will render you impeccable. You can't spare two minutes? Then fold it neatly and place it in the mending basket in the corner of your bedroom—any receptacle with some basic sewing supplies tucked inside it will suffice. But lest out of sight become out of mind, be sure to carry the basket with you whenever you settle down in front of the TV. That way the three of you—the tube, the mending, and you—can enjoy engrossingly productive hours together. And you, my dear, will ever appear meticulously attired.

Your "short" genes (you're welcome!) have added a little something extra to your life. It's called the hem. I've harped on it enough that you must know by now, there is no shortcut to a decent-looking hem. It must be measured, trimmed, and inconspicuously sewn or it's conspicuously ugly. If you lack time and patience, find someone who has it—and who sews and is willing to do it for love or money—such as your mother or a seamstress. A miniature sewing kit plus a couple of safety pins, always carried in your purse, will save your life you know not when.

Do I need to remind you, Cathy, that monochromatic outfits will not chop you shorter the way boldly contrasting ones will? You'll look taller and skinnier in skirts, slacks, and tops of identical or blending colors. Horizontal stripes are a menace. They can make even tall people look like squashed accordions. Plaids are for schoolgirls or for those who are daring enough not to care how broad they look—unless you are lucky enough to run across one of the subdued rarities done in soft, muted colors.

Except on an occasional therapeutic wild spree, resist all those ravishing fun prints. They'll no longer be fun after the third wearing. Your friends will think you own nothing else no matter how infrequently you wear them. Plain colors are eternally repeatable. A few changes of accessories will keep you well dressed in the same dress for years with no one, except you, being the wiser.

Invest in a couple of good outfits for daily wear. For festive flings, shop the bargain stores. A party dress has had it once you've been seen in it. If accosted by an overly persuasive salesclerk, "think about it" politely and go to another store.

Be extremely wary, hon, of buying end-of-the-season fads as bargains. Almost without exception, the better bargain is the fashion that's on its way in, not out. But what normal red-blooded American woman can resist a "real bargain"? So when you must, go ahead and buy it and when you come to your senses, give it away.

Once or twice a year, pull your least favorites out of your closet and pass them along to some charitable organization. Do it while they're still sufficiently stylish to bring some pleasure to someone else. It feels good.

When was the last time you polished your shoes? Aha, gotcha, didn't I? Shoe polishing was a Saturday night ritual at our house when I was growing up. It would have been unthinkable to start for church in the morning in scruffy shoes. Grandpa saw to that! Maybe that's why squeaky-clean shoes have always seemed to me to be almost as important as squeaky-clean hair.

Granpa was the only person I ever heard of back then who washed his hair every day. It was jet black and glistened as he moved. I didn't appreciate how ahead of his time his routine was. The child never does until later.

Dazzling white shirts with their collars and cuffs starched cardboard stiff were another Grandpa idiosyncrasy. He went through about three a day. The first half of Grandma's week was devoted to doing them to perfection. She used a washboard and tub and a big copper boiler. There were no steam irons and starch scorched readily. (Does this explain why I won't buy clothes that require a lot of ironing?)

Clothes were always sprinkled, then rolled up to distribute the dampness throughout them before they were ironed. Even with today's instant spray starches the result is better if they're done that way.

The most expensive clothing can look nondescript if it's not carried erectly. So if you glance in a store window and see a reflection of someone who is sagging or slouching, quick, sign up for a ballet class! Meanwhile—head up, sternum high, ear tops to ceiling, earlobes over shoulders, elbows down to waist. These quick checkpoints will realign everything, including a protruding stomach. Every so often, observe your own walk. It is always something of a shock to me when the reflection in the store window looks nothing like the one in my head. Unattractive habits can make themselves at home without your having the slightest idea they're there.

I mean it about the ballet class—or some similar activity like yoga or general toning or some combination. Too tired or too busy is no excuse. A physical regimen will move the cobwebs out of your brain as well as your body. How else do you expect to grow to be a spritely little old lady?

There is no self-indulgence more gratifying than to get "the works" at a good salon. The plain old you who entered leaves feeling like a princess because, it seems after all that, surely you must look like one. It feels go-o-o-d!

Meanwhile, all is not lost. Your trusty kitchen and bathroom cabinets are brimming with cheap goodies, ever-ready to keep you beautiful and young forever. Kidding? I certainly am not! Before manufacturers took over the job, inventiveness kept us beautiful. It still does, some of us. Here are some examples. In order to . . .

- Add body to hair: Pour beer on it after shampooing, then rinse it out.

- Strengthen weak hair: Work whipped egg white into washed hair. Rinse it out.

- Condition hair: Work in about one half cup mayonnaise, wrap hair in a plastic bag for twenty minutes. Wash and rinse hair.

- Set and hold hair: Dissolve one tablespoon or more sugar in one half cup warm water. Apply with comb to roller-width sections of hair. Let dry. Keep flyswatter handy!

- Cream face: Prick a vitamin E capsule and smear on contents. Especially good for eye and mouth area lines. . . . or
  . . . rub on some cocoa butter. Pregnant ladies prevented stretch marks by melting, then rubbing on expanding areas. I have three children, no stretch marks. Keep a chocolate bar handy. The smell awakens cravings.
  . . . or
  . . . snap an inch or two off a leaf of your aloe plant. Smear on the oozing liquid. A good make-up foundation and mild sunscreen. Also good for stove and sunburns.

- Create a facial masque: Scoop a spoonful of sour cream or yogurt (almost as good) out of carton and slather on generously. Let dry for twenty minutes or so. Rinse off with lukewarm water . . . or
. . . whip until thick, an egg yolk (left over from hair treatment), a teaspoon of honey, a scant teaspoon of lemon juice. Cover face with generous quantity. Let dry twenty minutes or more. Rinse with lukewarm water. The "goop" lasts a week in the refrigerator.

- Maintain complexion: In a small jar combine equal quantities (approximately) of liquid vitamin E, glycerin, distilled water, and aloe gel (drug counter items, all). Shake vigorously and apply with fingertips.

- Tighten complexion: Once over face lightly with an ice cube or cold washcloth.

- Moisturize face: Dad's creamy after-shave lotion. Hasn't grown whiskers yet.

With all the money you've saved going natural you can go on that Caribbean cruise . . . and let a smile flicker briefly as you hear them whisper, "Who's that stunning stranger?" Bon voyage, cherie!

9   Dating

Dating? Hum-mm Cathy, this little old lady is so far out of step with today that for once she is speechless. . . . But at the same time she is confident that anyone adult enough to earn her own living and create her own lifestyle, unassisted, knows what's best for whatever or whoever may turn up in her life. The parental yearning to shield our young from any potential heartbreak lingers, no matter what the age of the child. So, kid, just keep your zippers zipped, your buttons buttoned, and have a good time. Look what dating did for me!

10 Health

It's not age that causes the graying of parents. It's panic . . . panic that this job they've stumbled into is bigger than they are . . . panic that they're groping their way through something they know nothing about . . . panic that the child who just threw up on the carpet won't recover to do it again next week. Sickness, that's the biggie. Once parents have survived a night with a sick child, forever after, that child's life is doomed to:

> ". . . and put on your rubbers. Don't forget your mittens. How many times have I told you not to go out with a wet head? Get in this minute; are you *trying* to catch a cold? . . ."

It's enough to make a child sick—do you remember? We weren't saying it for *our* health, you know. Even though you are no longer under our roof, everything about you still matters. So do us a favor, sweetie. Stay healthy.

One of the easiest things you can do for yourself is get plenty of rest. Watching a late night show, then stumbling out of bed still half asleep early the next morning will not enhance your productivity or your health. Get in the habit of sprinkling five-minute breaks throughout your workday, giving your mind and your body a chance to slip into neutral and regenerate for the tasks still ahead. If I was able to figure out a way to do it with young children under foot, you can manage it in the office. It will help you keep your perspective.

Now that your mother is not there to monitor your nourishment, who's in charge? I don't know anyone who eats carefully enough to fulfill each day's nutritional requirements. When you girls were growing up, I practically chained myself to the kitchen trying. Then when you turned up your noses at what was on your plates, I was sure that you would never reach adulthood healthy—and it would be my fault. All the homemaker, in those days, heard from the experts was, "Each meal *must* contain something from each of the four basic food groups." Well, experts, schmexperts! I wonder how many of them practiced what they preached.

Eventually I became brave enough to serve my family four basics per day instead of per meal. And renegade that I have become as I approach the twilight, I try to work them in once a week. Eating from one food group one day and another the next hasn't had any adverse effect that I have noticed—have you?

The nutritional essentials seem to be vitamins, and they need to be taken as supplements because what we eat normally doesn't provide enough.

I'm sure, without even asking, that the copy of Dr. Linus Pauling's book, *How to Live Longer and Feel Better* (W. H. Freeman & Co., New York), which I sent you is lying, still barely glanced-at, somewhere in your apartment. Even if the title excited you, which I doubt it did, the conditioned child-to-parent response is, "Okay, Mom, just a minute." I understand: The parent was the child in an earlier life.

So, to save you time and spare you guilt, here's what Dr. Pauling says in chapter two of his book:

> To secure my recommended intakes of supplementary vitamins and minerals . . . I take only four tablets a day. These are one 800-IU vitamin E capsule, one super-B tablet, one vitamin and mineral tablet, and one 25,000-IU vitamin A capsule. I take them in the evening. I take much of my vitamin C in the morning, before breakfast, 12 g (three level teaspoonfuls) of pure crystalline ascorbic acid either dissolved in orange juice to buffer it or in water with a small amount of baking soda . . . added to make an effervescent drink . . . At this writing, in the year 1985, the four tablets I take every day plus the 18 g of vitamin C (L-ascorbic acid, fine crystals) . . . need cost you only as much as one small chocolate bar.

There! What's so complicated about that? Four tablets plus a couple of glasses of vitamin C-laced liquid a day. Think you can handle that?

You know how I feel about exercise, so I'll lay off (this time) and move on to an aspect of health you do wonder about: "How long does food stay good so it won't make me sick?" Right? As a general rule, with certain exceptions, freeze what you won't eat in the next two or three days. Throw out what's still around then. Prepared foods from a restaurant or deli should be discarded if not eaten the day after you brought them home. Provided it was fresh when you originally put it in the freezer (or was solidly frozen at the time), you usually can refreeze an item once assuming it has not sat out of the refrigerator at room temperature in its thawed state or in the refrigerator that way.

A homemade soup or stew should be good for about a week in the refrigerator. Smell it. Taste it. Throw it out if it doesn't look, smell, or taste right. Home-cooked chicken, promptly and carefully refrigerated, should be good for three or four days. If the fish was fresh when you cooked it, day after tomorrow would be max, depending on smell and texture, which changes if it's "going."

Here's a related for-instance: On the way home from work you buy some fresh

chicken, but you don't feel like cooking. Next day, realizing you'll be working late, you put it in your freezer. A month later, experiencing a "chicken attack," you transfer the frozen chicken into the refrigerator to thaw so you can cook it for dinner. Meanwhile, wonder of wonders, that cute guy from the front office invites you to dinner. Question: What to do with the thawed chicken? Answer: Beats me! Nah, not altogether. If it were I and I didn't get home too late from my date, I'd cook the chicken before going to bed, ice it down to cool it quickly, refrigerate it overnight, and in the morning refreeze the portion that I didn't expect to consume in the next couple of days.

It's hard to be exact about these things. They're "experience" decisions that take trial and error to learn. Mistakes are what taught me. In general, if it looks fresh, smells fresh, and its texture seems not to have changed, it should be safe to eat. Try a bite. If it tastes good, enjoy. If you're not sure, throw it out. A taste or two of something questionable shouldn't cause anything more serious than a mild case of the trots.

A bit of mold on cheese or on top of maple syrup may not mean you have to throw it all out. But why am I telling you all this? If you have a question about something specific, just call me—or some other experienced homemaker. Our guess may not be any better than yours, but at least you'll have the reassurance of a second opinion.

Hand washing is as good a health insurance policy as any I know. I wash mine constantly while I'm preparing food. I'm sure if more people were fastidious about it, germs would spread less freely. The general laxness about hand washing, (which I've noticed in public restrooms,) makes it even more important for you to do it. Frequent hand washing will help cut down the number of colds you pick up. Carry packets of hand-wipes as a precautionary measure.

A cold is nothing to sneeze at. If you wear boots and bundle up, you will not invite a cold. Another way to avoid a cold is not to kiss someone who has one. This is especially true if the person you are kissing has a runny nose and is coughing or sneezing. Of course, I don't know why you'd want to kiss such a person anyway, but young people don't see things the same way older folks do. They just exchange germs without even thinking what they are doing.

Of course, if you take your quota of vitamins every day, you may not catch the cold that's going around the office. Once you feel one coming on, though, load up on vitamin C. Take it every hour!

And don't forget the soup—lots of good, hot chicken soup. Homemade is best. But you don't have time. Working people can't come home to make a big

pot of soup. Just get yourself some canned broth. And keep a jar of bouillon granules in your desk. You can get hot water in the restroom, and keep sipping hot soup all day instead of coffee. Anyway, it's better for you.

Do you have a fresh lemon or a bottle of lemon juice? Add a teaspoon or two plus honey, to suit your taste, to a cup of hot tea. Drink it plenty hot. Doesn't just thinking about it remind you how good it used to feel trickling down a sore throat?

I know you don't think it helps, but putting a little mild mentholated ointment in your nostrils won't hurt. It will open up clogged breathing passages. Before there were throat sprays, we would lay a lump of ointment on our tongue to melt down our throat. Ugh, how I hated it!

My mother used to tell me, "Don't walk in the basement in bare feet or sit on cement; it will give you a cold now and rheumatism when you're older." I still follow her advice even though she has been gone many years. I also agree with her that no one living in a cold climate should go outdoors or to bed with wet hair.

If you soak your feet in hot water just before you get in bed, it's good for the circulation. (As our grandparents used to say, it's good for what ails you.) In the old days people used to put hot bricks in bed by their feet. Of course, they didn't have furnaces, bedrooms weren't heated, and houses turned into iceboxes at night. Dad's mother, I remember, always took a hot water bottle to bed for her feet. Grandpa fixed it for her—a rather touching nocturnal ritual.

It helps if you have someone sweet and thoughtful to bring you a hot water bottle, or whatever else you need when you're sick. That's when a husband would be mighty handy.

Of course, if *he* gets sick, that's something else. There's nothing worse than a man who is sick enough to feel rotten, but not sick enough to be in the hospital (there he purrs contentedly while a paid nurse rubs his back). The time I came closest to checking out on your father was when he caught chicken pox from you. That lovely man turned into a monster. He had me running and fetching until I nearly dropped. And *crabby.* But we were talking about colds.

Here are some old-fashioned remedies, you've probably never even heard of. For instance, did I ever tell you about my mother's favorite treatment when your Uncle Mike and I were little? She melted goose grease on the stove, rubbed it on our throats and wrapped them with a nice, warm flannel cloth. I heard just recently that the merits of goose grease are being rediscovered. Grandma also would give us warm milk to drink, flavored with garlic and tiny puddles of melted butter. Why are you laughing? Do you know that now scientists are saying garlic is good for all sorts of ailments including colds? And some doctors have finally acknowledged that chicken soup works. Of course, there's garlic in chicken soup, so that goes to show what smart people grandmothers really are. The world would be better off if we listened to our grandmothers.

And, hon, it is "feed a cold and starve a fever"—not the other way around. I hope this bit of ancient wisdom helps you stay healthier and recover faster if you ever get sick—which I hope you won't!

11 Work

Congratulations, Cathy, on making it into the most exclusive club in America: The Wage-Earner Club! It feels good, doesn't it, to get a paycheck for your efforts. When the school days end, the workdays begin. Have you detected a similarity between the two? All those years of classes, activities, practice, and chores have done their job.

Growing up conscientious is the stepping-stone to making it in a career. We hope yours will bring you both pleasure and success. Homework, piano, ballet, household chores, Girl Scout activities—all have left their imprint. Results are achieved by tedious tasks taken in stride. This is as true of keeping house and earning a living as it was of making it through school.

Success takes concentration; distraction is its enemy. At the office, avoid becoming a confidante of people who spend their workdays gossiping, chatting, and commiserating with one another. They can keep you from getting your work done and get you mixed up in things that are none of your business.

Steer clear of workplace chumminess, and you won't be tempted, in a weak moment, to share information that's no one else's business. Once a morsel has left your lips, there's no retrieving it and no telling where it may eventually land.

When emotion or anger stirs you beyond all reason, go ahead and sound off; pour your heart out—but do it in a letter. You can "let it all hang out" in the letter,

provided you do not mail it! No, no, no! Slip the letter, instead, into a desk or bureau drawer and do not even peek at it for twenty-four to forty-eight hours. By then you will have simmered down enough to reread the letter with a clear head, not an addled one—and you can trust yourself to act sensibly instead of irrationally. Whether you're addressing your boyfriend or your boss or some business matter, it's all the same.

Those who continually criticize their boss or their company should find work somewhere else. While they are paying you, your employers are entitled to your loyalty and your cooperation. A smart dog does not bite the hand that feeds it. Doing something to lessen or to solve a problem is better than crabbing about it. Anyone can crab—effective employees contribute to the solution. Feeling resentful will interfere with your work and make you sick. That's not fair to your employer or yourself.

Wage earners and homemakers who enjoy their work must perform plenty of

tiresome tasks. Why, even Beethoven had to practice scales before he could create beautiful music. Young homemakers and workers who appreciate this aren't nearly as bored with scrubbing the toilet at home or filing last week's conference reports at the office. Every job has boring parts.

There is dignity and merit in every job, as anyone can tell you who has experienced the inconvenience of uncollected garbage or malfunctioning plumbing. It's a pity this isn't emphasized more to our schoolchildren.

If the physical work of keeping school buildings and yards tidy and attractive could be part of every child's education, fewer of them would deface public places. Unfortunately, societies that are more repressive than ours appear to do a better job than we of teaching respect for physical work. In some countries, children are required to perform some farm, janitorial, and public parks services. What child (or community) wouldn't benefit from experiencing what goes into bringing food to the table, maintaining our schools, and preserving our parks? In time we might all become more conscientious about leaving where we are, better for the next person who's going to be there.

Jobs, like children, make better progress if they're nudged along with big helpings of love. This means that if you can't change your job, you must change the way you feel about it. The positive approach is a great transformer. Dad and I hope that, for you, your career will turn out to be a labor of love.

12 Paychecks

Next to the pleasure of doing work you enjoy is the pleasure of getting paid for it. Usually what you get is a paycheck. But is the paycheck only a monetary illusion? You work hard. You earn it. You cash it. And, poof—it's gone. What happens? Where is *your* paycheck now?

Did it float into someone's cash register and all you have to show for it are baubles that might better have been unbought? Or is your waistline bulging from irresistibles that might better have been resisted? Or were gifts lavished upon someone to whom you now scarcely speak? Or has some video game, concert, film, or other diversion gulped a goodly chunk of last month's earnings?

Contemporary entertainment has become outrageously expensive. Much of it is also questionably entertaining.

Too often, at outlandish admission prices, movie theaters show nothing better than naked people who aren't married to each other rolling around together in the same bed. Years ago, it took talent to be in films. Rolling and panting don't require any talent at all. If you've seen one of each kind of body, you've seem them all. The parts are the same. But I suppose providing bedsheets is cheaper for moviemakers than dressing actors in extravagant costumes like we used to pay a quarter to see in lavish, talent-crammed productions. It appears to me that surviving from one paycheck to the next takes more talent than is visible on many of today's cinema screens.

Survival suggestion number one: remove from each paycheck whatever you can *save.* Lock it up in an account where it can grow. Yes, I know I'm nagging, but it's hard for people your age to understand that youth is not a perpetual condition. Who knows what will have happened to Social Security by the time it's your turn? Survivors anticipate problems and plan alternatives. They don't wait to be taken care of.

Survival suggestion number two: say "no" to yourself. "No" is critical when you are in a store full of pretty clothing designed for lifestyles other than yours. "Yes" will give you a closet full of garments, but "nothing to wear." Say "no" if it won't complete, improve, or replace something you already own. Closets are graveyards for unmated separates. Say "no" if it's a bouncy print you'll be sick of in a month. Say "no" if it begs to be bought but you really don't need it. At the moment, the "no" may hurt but it will feel so-o-o good later!

As a resourceful person, be alert for other ways to survive from paycheck to

paycheck. You can see a matinee for half the price of an evening performance, or wait a couple of weeks and see it at the dollar movie theater. Weekend afternoons are ideal for seeing shows. When you're unescorted, that's safer anyhow.

Eat in nice restaurants at noon. The same menu most likely costs more at night, as much as double! You'll feel less conspicuous lunching than dining alone. Brown bagging some lunches can help you afford it.

All of this is leading up to quiet evenings at home, isn't it? But your money is going farther and you are not exposing yourself to needless personal risk. In many areas, women can venture out safely after dark only in packs, like animals. This is freedom, and survival, in the eighties.

Don't write any check until you first record it in your check register. Enter the date, the sequence number of the check, to whom, how much, and in some instances, what for. *Then* write the check. If you didn't subtract the amount as you recorded it, do it as soon as you get home. In your register, ignore the deposits section. It's worthless. Instead, when you add money to your account, enter it in sequence in the register, following the last check you wrote. Add the deposit to that balance. When your monthly statement comes, cross off each canceled check with a pencil mark in your register as well as on the statement. You and the bank should come close to agreeing. If you consistently don't, spend some time with your friendly banker and learn how to do it their way. Or, try your old trick: change banks.

I take it for granted, of course, that (ahem!) you very carefully saved all your charge purchase slips from last month. Good for you! You squirreled them, for safekeeping, into an envelope marked for that purpose. Now, when your statement arrives correlate each one with the itemized list and cross it off. Save any

purchase slips which might be needed as proof of purchase and staple them to your retained portion of the statement. Then pay the bill.

Notify (a phone call can usually expedite it) anyone who appears to have made a mistake, whether it's in their favor or yours. It's pretty safe to go ahead and write a check after that. They'll credit you if it's their error. Devote one evening a month to this sort of thing. Managing your money is your business.

You must pay your bills promptly and not spend more than you earn. You must save something—no matter how little—out of every paycheck for devastating unexpected expenses. Impossible? No. Pretend you didn't even see the money. You not only can, but you must do it.

When you're buying something costly, like a piece of furniture, you may be able to take advantage of a payment option called "ninety days same as cash." It's worth asking about because it permits you to take up to three months to pay for the item without its costing you a penny of interest. If that option is not available at the store where you are trading, another payment-stretching plan may be. Stores don't always volunteer such customer benefits; they'd rather get paid immediately or charge you a hefty interest on a balance due.

Another seldom broadcast but nice-for-the-customer policy of quality department stores (and perhaps others, as well) is a willingness to adjust the regular price of an item to its sale price if you purchase it within two weeks of when it goes on sale. It's a good reason for trading at reliable stores. They also graciously accept returned items—in good condition, of course.

Any time you have a grievance concerning a service or payment or purchase

or whatever, keep after it until it's resolved to your satisfaction. If a phone call doesn't result in an immediate correction, start a letter-writing campaign. It may take months, in stubborn cases, and a barrage of letters, but polite persistence on your part should, in time, straighten out the mess. Computers, like people, are not infallible, and it's your money. Often a company, honest though it may be, seems not to have any idea what its computer is up to.

I suppose I am out of step with the times, but I would not trust an automatic teller money machine with my banking. Computers are like some men. They are perfectly wonderful, but they are "never wrong." No matter how a computer, or such a man, goofs up, it's always your fault. A computer, however, will never whisper, "I'm sorry," with a bouquet of roses.

If you treat your obligations and your paycheck with respect, you will be labeled a good credit risk. Such a designation will come in handy when needed, such as if you want to borrow money from the bank to purchase a car.

A lot of fine print comes with every charge card issued. Examine it carefully before you sign up, and cancel promptly (by letter) if anything about it doesn't suit you. Things to watch for, especially, are how much interest is charged, and how it is determined and computed. What you learn may shock you. Here's one that shook me:

Dad and I try to pay the full balance due on our account each month so we won't have to pay any interest (yes, at times I practice what I preach), so I was appalled to find an interest charge on one of our statements. When I phoned to challenge it, the reason given was that this particular bank now charged interest on the interval between when they paid a merchant and when they received our monthly check. It was an outrageous way for the bank to "double dip" since our having the account with them had already given them reason to collect a percentage of the purchase price from the merchant. Needless to say, I lost no time in cancelling that account.

It takes vigilance, Cathy, to hang on to the buck you have worked so hard to earn.

13 Economizing

Use it once and throw it away—throw it away—throw it away. What a convenience! Right? For your generation, sure. For mine—well, we've been conditioned by a thriftier time . . . the time of the great Depression. When convenience of the moment bids me: throw it away, a little voice out of my past whispers, "Depression. What if there's another one?" They're not publicized in advance like new movies.

Nobody will come through town on a horse yelling, "The depression is coming." It just happens. One morning you wake up and there it is. No jobs. No money. Nowhere to turn. Banks go broke; the government, too. A depression is frightening enough to scare wastefulness out of you for a lifetime. I hope you will never have to live through one.

A depression can make a miser out of a spendthrift. And that's not all bad. The habit of economizing stretches your salary leaving you with the price of lunch for two rather than in debt before payday.

And what's so wrong, young lady, with rinsing out plastic bags, plastic cups, plastic spoons, and the like? What I don't use, my granddaughters can play with when they visit! A coffee filter rinsed is one less to buy. Little things add up. As for twist ties, it's simply a convenience to find a few used ones when you have misplaced those that came with the package of plastic bags. You were a Girl Scout once. Wasn't "Be Prepared" your motto?

Speaking of which, do you remember what we used to do with old nylon stockings back in the days when you were making stuffed dolls and animals as scout projects? The stockings were laundered, of course, and used as stuffing for the toys you made to give away at Christmas. If we were still doing that sort of thing, I'd have old nylons coming out of my ears. They make perfect stuffing—soft, lump-free, washable, and very handy.

By the way, do you remember my reason for always buying two of any shade of panty hose? After one leg of each has sprung a run, I can make a third pair by combining the remaining good legs.

Another use we made of old nylons was to cut off a length of the leg and stuff it with dried flower petals from the bouquets various boyfriends had sent you.

These made fragrant sachets to tuck into drawers or hang in the closet. You didn't think it was so funny then; why are you laughing now? If you threw away less, you could be laughing you way through a movie instead of turning pockets inside out searching for coins.

It seems that everything that is needed for anything can be purchased, used once, and thrown away. But even when the cost is just pennies per item, the pennies add up to a dollar you no longer have. When you want a dust cloth, you run to the store and buy a package of them. We made ours out of worn clothing and linens. They weren't as pretty as today's store-bought, but so what? Ours did the job, didn't cost a penny, and were always available without an excursion to the store.

If you should ever want to try homemade cleaning rags, today's all-cottons, especially knits like old T-shirts, would be perfect. Bedsheets once made great rags, but not now! Most of them now are blended with synthetic yarns for wrinkle resistance. This makes them unsuitable for rags, but a godsend for beds. We used to iron the all-cotton sheets. Imagine! Wool, though, is marvelous for polishing furniture and shoes. Even if you stick with store-bought cloths, where does it say you can use them only once? They'll last through several rinsings.

Clear plastic dry cleaner bags can keep out-of-season clothes dustfree and easy to locate. They crumple into soft packing material for mailing gifts. It's wasteful not to reuse them. I don't know how many times the brown paper grocery bags I've saved have come in handy for wrapping packages for mailing. With gift wrap getting prettier and costlier, it's harder than ever to throw any away if it can be ironed to brighten another gift. The ribbons, I must admit, are harder to recycle. They tend to stick to the bottom of the iron.

The old admonition "waste not, want not" makes more sense than ever now that some of our natural resources are becoming depleted. I'm too conservation conscious to waste water and electricity on a partial dishwasher load. With just Dad and me at home, I use our machine mostly after company. Whether they go into the dishwasher or the dishpan, our dishes get the food scrubbed off their faces with a brush first. Some things never see the inside of the dishwasher because it ruins wood, chips crystal, pits silver, and melts certain plastics. Nevertheless, I wouldn't want to give up ours, and I'm glad you have one, too.

Sometime, though, rather than run a minuscule load (the same amount of water is wasted whether the landlord pays for it or you; same goes for electricity) try letting your dishes soak themselves clean in hot soapsuds, rinse them off later, and by morning you'll find them as ready to use out of your sink drainer as out of the dishwasher. The amount of work is about the same, but the resource saving is considerable.

For a little variety, mix your own soda beverages. Make them of unsugared fruit juices, club soda, and ice cubes.

Has it occurred to you lately that you're a taxpayer now? Think about it when you're about to run out to buy another book or magazine. There's a library sitting in your neighborhood. It's full of books and publications for you to enjoy free for the borrowing. You can borrow even current bestsellers by putting your name on a waiting list.

As for records, tapes, and movies, many libraries lend those, too. Some libraries even lend framed artwork. You'll be surprised at the variety of goodies you can borrow. If you haven't been there lately, stop by the library. It's been long enough since your last research paper that you can be friends again. Buying everything you read adds up.

I don't know what made me think of it now but one way you don't ever want

to economize is by hanging on to cracked china. Unless it's great grandma's strictly ornamental Haviland, throw it out. The cracks are traps for germs. Refuse any restaurant food served on a cracked plate or in a cracked cup. Ugh!

Popular periodicals are filled with imaginative ideas for creating new things out of old ones. What they seldom mention is the cost, the mess, and the time it takes to do the converting. It makes a nice living for the writers and busy work for people with time on their hands. But such projects are not for the present likes of you. She who has plenty to do pursuing a career is better off letting charities have her old things and buying what she needs ready-made or hand-made by others.

Much the same is true of home maintenance. Why not just concentrate on earning enough at your specialty so you can afford to hire plumbers, carpenters, and cleaning people to do theirs? You'd certainly be saving time and, probably, money. Too often do-it-yourself is an expensive way to economize.

14 Giving

"Help your neighbor" is what this country is all about. Brave individuals tackled wildernesses until, working in unison, they managed to create a country with a heart of gold. Having come from diverse backgrounds from which they may have been driven by hunger or oppression, Americans continue, today, to remember. Generations later, the pioneer spirit of pitch-in-and-help lives on and makes our nation the most responsive to need world-wide.

Americans . . . giving . . . why, they go together like bread and butter . . . or like you're supposed to think of mom and apple pie. So what if the pie comes from the grocer's deep freeze? It's the giving that counts, and today's young moms give plenty! Juggling jobs and families and homes, they give it all—then wonder why they're so tired.

We grow up expecting to support our church or synagogue plus certain other good causes. That comes as naturally as expecting, eventually, to put our children through school. It's the "others," beyond such groups as the United Way and the Red Cross, who approach us with their urgent appeals that make it so difficult to know where to pull up and say, "Whoa!"

So many deserving groups now exist that our mailboxes bulge with pleas for help. Much of what is collected must be used to cover the cost of collecting it, with the needy getting only the leftovers. This does not diminish the worthiness, of course, of any cause, but does make it imperative to budget your giving as carefully as you budget your rent and car payments. Otherwise, you'll respond to one heartrending appeal after another and find yourself without lunch money by the end of the month. The professionals who make a career of appealing to our innate compassion for our fellow man know how to present needs very convincingly. Their salaries depend on it.

Beyond the normal obligations to church, family, and community, the first thing is to decide which causes you truly *wish* to support. Then, figure, realistically, how much money or time you can spare for them. Confine *all* your giving within these limits. This can take as much discipline as dieting. But you will feel better for having given thoughtfully rather than haphazardly. So will your chosen charities.

Clothing and household items in usable condition will always find another home, thanks to such organizations as the Red Cross, Salvation Army, St. Vincent de Paul Society, Goodwill, and others. But if you can pass your things along in a condition which makes them a pleasure to receive . . . well, that's all the better.

It is not a sin to say, "No, thanks," to soliciting door-to-door for some worthy group. Nor need you feel obligated to the neighbor who stops at your door for a contribution unless you are already planning to give. The need won't vanish because you choose to reflect on it overnight or to give at another time.

Gifts which arrive unsolicited asking for donations do not require any reply. Neither the gift nor any cash need be returned. Don't ever feel guilty about ignoring merchandise you did not request.

If the phone rings and someone asks you to buy something for whatever cause, worthy or not, in your sweetest, politest voice say, "Thank you for calling, but I never respond to phone solicitations." If the caller persists, add, "It's against my principles," and quietly hang up. For goodness sake, *never, never* give a stranger *any* information (even if just, supposedly, responding to a survey) about yourself on the phone. If someone has hired the caller to do this, as is usually the case, that's his problem. He should find a different job.

Toward the end of the year, after you have met all your obligations and put aside enough for your year-end and April taxes, that's the time to do something nice for some additional deserving cause. If you're giving to accredited organizations, you will want to keep a record of this for tax purposes. Always contribute by check, not cash.

Your first responsibility is to provide well enough for your own needs that you won't ever have to be taken care of by society or anyone else. Many people don't have the privilege of such an option, so it's up to the rest of us to do what we can. What better way than by voluntarily sharing can we inch our way toward making this *one* world?

15   Traveling

Traveling is fun. And beautifying. If you travel a lot you will have pretty arms because lugging suitcases will give you muscles where your stay-at-home friends get flab.

Some things about traveling are a pain in the neck, though, such as getting ready to go. That's the hard part. But, being there soon makes up for that. It's sort of like having a baby. The joy of having it makes you forget the misery that went before. And once you have actually filled and fastened your suitcase, the feeling is much the same.

Figuring out what to put into the suitcase, though, is enough to make you wish you were staying home. Don't. Staying home will get you nowhere. Just pack. Doing it is easier than thinking about it. Can't make yourself face up to it? I've finally broken through that one; I trick myself with an artificial departure date and try to convince my brain to believe it. It's surprising how gullible I am and how effectively it works.

To help visualize what you will need, pretend you are going for only three days, no matter how long your trip really will be. In that case, all you really *need* is:

—an outfit to travel in (including raincoat and umbrella),

—an outfit to change into when you get there,

—a fresh outfit for the next day, and,

—your nightie and grooming necessities.

Any needs beyond that you can buy at your destination. If you arrive with your bag only half full (or with a spare empty one), you can indulge yourself shamelessly at all sorts of quaint little shops and bring home a bulging suitcase, an empty wallet, and a clear conscience. And you'll have useful souvenirs instead of just knickknacks.

Do you know what you should *not* pack? Anything that won't drip-dry overnight! Unless you plan to take your mother along to do the ironing, you'd better leave all that natural fiber stuff in your closet. Polyester is God's gift to travelers. Why, before synthetics even our underwear had to be ironed. Undergarments were no less important then than now. Fast-drying, wrinkle-free fabrics make it easier, though, to look nice where it doesn't show.

Of course, Cathy, you always carry a sturdy purse over your shoulder with one hand firmly gripping it and you never leave it unzipped—right? That's good!

I felt sure you'd say yes. In addition to the usual billfold items, do you keep a concealed emergency-only ten-dollar bill, plus coins for a phone call? Conceal them inside your shoe from purse-snatchers or pickpockets. What repeated life-savers they've been for me.

In addition to the usual little accordion-folded rain hood, I try to carry a couple of quart-size plastic bags. Why? Oh, lots of reasons. What if there's a downpour? They make great emergency galoshes with a rubber band slipped over each ankle. There are plenty of ways a handy plastic bag can save the day.

Another lifesaver is my tiny penknife, with its scissors, nail file, and corkscrew. It has saved many a day for me and for fellow travelers, as have my miniature measuring tape, sewing kit, and safety pins. Scotch tape can hold up a hem temporarily and de-lint you, sticky side out. For restroom repairs, a travel tooth-brush and dental floss are handbag handies. Women are luckier than men; they can carry all these necessities in a bag slung over their shoulder (remembering, of course, to switch shoulders regularly). Especially when traveling, it's convenient to have your necessities always at hand.

One more use for the trusty plastic bag: put your shoes in them so they can't soil anything else you've packed, especially when you're going city to city, making one-night stops. And shoes hold their shape better en route if you stuff them with such things as stockings, socks, rolled belts, etc.

Roll up your clothing like jelly rolls. Roll-packing saves space and keeps things from wrinkling so much. A large tube of shampoo concentrate will keep your hair and your clothing fresh until you get home. You can find laundromats even in foreign countries, so why carry clothing you're not sure you'll need?

By all means, don't carry any valuable jewelry. If you don't lose it, someone may be tempted to take it plus heaven knows what else along with it. It's up to you not to put temptation before weak-willed strangers.

You've never felt as ignorant as you'll feel the day you try to pay for something in a foreign country with money you don't recognize or understand. They *always* know not only their money, but ours as well—at least so it seems! So, if you're going to another country, order some of that country's money from your local bank. It takes about a week. Practice with it at home. Then you can arrive abroad smart, smug, and confident—or at least able to pay your cabdriver.

And while we're on money, carry plenty of dollar bills and quarters or their foreign equivalents. Almost everyone who does anything for you while you travel will expect (and frequently deserve) a tip. Gratuity money disappears so fast, it's like feeding popcorn to pigeons. Every time you turn around, you need more. Being taken care of doesn't come cheap.

Are you aware, Cathy, that most foreign hotels don't furnish washcloths—just towels? Put one of your hotel's matchbooks in your purse. That way you'll have the address and phone number if you need it. This is especially handy for communicating with non-English-speaking cabdrivers. Also, a matchbook cover stuck into the chain lock slot of your door will help thwart anyone trying to slip the chain to get into your room.

Whenever practical, walk so you are walking toward oncoming traffic instead of in the same direction. That makes it harder for some evil-minded stranger to grab you and force you into his car. It's unfair but true that the safest thing a woman can do for herself is be hard to get.

Carry a small notebook to jot the names of people and places you want to recall when you get home. After the day's clothing is drip-drying in the bathroom and before you turn out the light, review the day's expenses and jot them down in the same notebook. It will help you stay solvent until you get home. Take a hotel envelope and stuff into it the receipt from every purchase you make. This is especially helpful when bringing purchases through customs.

Of course, you'll talk to lots of strangers while you travel. How else can you meet interesting people wherever you go? Just keep your wits about you as you do it. Even your father and I were strangers once.

Girls driving convertibles worry me. What's to keep some weirdo from jumping in? *Never* leave your car unlocked even for a minute. *Always* glance behind the driver's seat to make sure no one is crouching there. And *never* pick up a hitchhiker no matter how safe he or she may look.

If you start getting sleepy while driving, massage your head and neck with one hand, then the other, until you reach an exit where you can pull off and rest. Blasts of fresh air help, too.

I'm finally convinced beyond any doubt that the most a driver can save by exceeding the speed limit is about a half hour in a day's driving time. I don't think this is worth risking a life or a neck, do you?

Don't forget your vitamins, sweetie. It takes plenty of energy to go places.

16 Clutter

Clutter can sneak up on a person as easily as installment payments or excess pounds. It's as hard to get rid of, too. It fills your closet, your desk, your cupboards. But even worse, it fills your time. (You're well aware, I'm sure, of the wrestling match I've had with it for years.)

How about you, hon, are you bogged down in paper instead of reading a good book? Are you glued to the telephone instead of romping with your dog? Are you paralyzed about what to wear when your closet is bulging with options? Are your evenings crammed with meetings when you would welcome a few delicious hours of nothing to do? See what I mean?

Clutter can be hard to recognize because it slips into your days so temptingly disguised that not until you find yourself gasping for free moments does it dawn on you that you no longer have a minute to call your own.

You agree to serve on a committee. No big deal. But before you know it, your phone is so tied up your boyfriend can't get through to invite you to a movie. Your weekends are promised to projects of minimal merit, at least insofar as they're of any real value to you.

That talkative girl at the next desk stops to confide her latest personal problems, and you carry home a briefcase full of the day's unfinished work.

Your friend drops off his laundry and parks himself for the evening in front of your TV. He has become such a fixture, you've lost the incentive to find a replacement.

You flip on the tube and are drawn into one absurd sitcom after another while the correspondence yellows in stacks on your desk.

It's endless, Cathy. You invite friends over for what you intended to be a simple dinner, which then proceeds to eat up your next three days. How do we do this to ourselves?

One way we could escape from it all would be to shuffle off to the Himalayas with nothing but a robe, prayer beads, and sandals. But I don't think we need to go that far, do you?

If you would like to try something that works pretty well for me, get yourself a large month-at-a-glance calendar with big blocks of white space. Mark everything on it that you know about ahead of time for the whole year, including birthdays, anniversaries, etc. Then, as more immediate things-to-do surface, pencil them in. You're busy if the calendar says, "Read book so and so." You're busy if it says, "Soak in bubble bath and manicure toenails."

Write in: review next season's wardrobe. Write in: the class in conversational Chinese you have put off for five years and the trip to the zoo that gets postponed from summer to summer.

You don't have to do everything you wrote in. Ignore what is no longer appealing when its time arrives—but at least you will have taken a first step toward uncluttering.

We-e-ell, maybe you have, and maybe you haven't because look what the postman just brought—a truckload of clippings from your mother. Whee! Just what you need, right? You may not agree but *she* (and I believe every word) is convinced that reading them will enhance the quality of your life and make you a candidate for sainthood. So not because you particularly want to, but because you love the old dear—and you know she'll ask about it when she phones tomorrow—you read them. Now what? It would be sacrilegious to deposit them in the wastebasket; they're from your mother.

Relax, hon, this old scissors-carrying clippings clipper is about to save your life (and her own as well). I have just read and sent on to you a copy of a marvelous little book by Pat Dorf. It's called *File ... Don't Pile!* (Willowtree Press). I think it's our answer. Happy uncluttering!

17   Standards

Standards, m'dear, are the invisible lines you draw around yourself. Without your having to say it in so many words, they let others know what you will and will not tolerate—what you expect of them; what they, in turn, can expect of you. Standards are pretty much the masters of your goals and achievements.

Whether you're the office doormat or on top of your workload—standards set you up for whichever it is. And when others work for you, it's your standards up to which they must perform.

Many tasks deserve no more than a lick and a promise. Don't give them any more. Reserve your earnest effort for the challenging jobs, then have fun really digging in. There's no point in giving any decent assignment only half a loaf when a full one is so much more satisfying.

Whether you participate in the office dirty jokes contest or walk away from the participants, it's up to your standards. Likewise the gossip pool which you can join or shun.

Standards make a difference in the way things go for you, hon. Keep the flag flying!

18 Responsibilities

The rent, the bills, the work, the responsibilities—yours are gearing up; ours are winding down—a fascinating cycle. As your generation says, "the beat goes on." It starts in childhood and never totally ends. Responsibility is a lifelong companion.

And a welcome companion it is! When Puffy, a tiny black and white ball of a kitten, greeted you on your fifth birthday, who could think of her as anything but fun? The pleasure she brought far outweighed any work she created, especially for you, as you poured her milk with stars in your eyes. She was yours to take care of!

Now, as you pursue your career, with stars in your eyes, Dad and I take much pleasure in watching you assume your new responsibilities.

You certainly have no need to be reminded that if you try to give your employer his money's worth and more, you'll be entrusted with work that will lead to greater reward. The clock does not tell a good worker, "Oops, gotta run." His or her own standards do that. When the job is done right, that's when to quit; your own enthusiasm for what you're doing sustains the momentum. You're responsible for the quality of what you produce, and entitled to the glow of satisfaction that comes of knowing you've done it well.

But, sweetie, your boss is not the most important person to whom you owe a responsibility. No, that person is y-o-u.

How much more preaching can you swallow about sensible, nourishing food? You need at least one wholesome, balanced meal plus some nourishing snacks each day. You need enough sleep to keep you alert and effective at your work the next day. Skipping meals occasionally won't kill you. Neither will losing a night's sleep. But making a habit of either or both will lead to trouble. So there, I've said it again. Advertisers know that repetition makes messages sink in; they learned it from their mothers.

Even easier to neglect than food or sleep is something that is easy to put off indefinitely: exercise. A good workout is exhilarating. It stimulates body and brain and helps you keep a good grip on life.

Running, biking, walking, swimming, skiing, golf, tennis—do whatever tugs at you most and gets you moving. In addition, try to schedule some dance, calisthenics, aerobics, or yoga class on a regular basis. No matter how tired you feel from a day at the office, a physical change of pace can make you feel like new.

Of course, muscles that aren't used to working will protest with a few aches. Tolerate them as you persist in nudging them gently back into prime condition.

As a desk worker, you really need to watch it, Cathy, to avoid habitually stooped shoulders and slack stomach muscles which can, in time, give you lower back pain. The spine needs to be stretched and twisted and bent every

day; yoga exercises are a centuries-old way to do that. Inverted positions are especially good for complexion and hair. Five or ten minutes of legs higher than head is ever so refreshing. You could do that while you watch the evening news. I feel I helped prevent varicose veins during pregnancy by sleeping with my legs instead of my head on a pillow.

Give those hard-working eyes of yours a break with some exercises. Up, down, wideways, diagonally, and around clockwise and counter-clockwise, move just your eyes. Then alternate your gaze from near to far. See how grateful they'll feel that you did this for them.

So don't neglect you, hon, 'cause you love what you take care of and take care of what you love. You're worth it!

19   Five-Year Shake

Here's one that Dad and I just sort of floundered into some years ago. We've named it The Five-Year Shake. The name doesn't matter. Here's the how-to:

At least every five years, step back and take an objective look at yourself—and if shortcomings are what you see, give your life a shake.

If you're doing okay in your job but see yourself stalemated in it, make a serious effort to find something better (keeping the present job, meanwhile, of course).

If you like your job but just can't make ends meet, find a way to come to terms with that.

Is the person in your mirror anything like the ideal in your head? No? What better time to change that than now? It seems to happen that about every five years I get inspired to have a serious confrontation with my wardrobe. This could be the time to sign up for that glamour course.

What about the friendships you have formed? Are they what you hoped for or do you need a trip to the meadow to see what's grazing in the pasture?

Are you getting a touch edgy about being trapped in a part of the country that you don't find all that appealing? What's keeping you cemented in place? Pick up and go wherever the lure pulls strongest.

If your five-year look at yourself says, "Change!" for heaven's sake don't wait another five years to do it.

20 Attitude

Unless there's something wrong with you physically, Cathy, how you feel is your own choice. Things don't do you in. You do yourself in. You can choose to be happy or miserable—whichever you prefer. Your attitude makes the difference. If a calamity strikes, you can sift through the rubble to see what new opportunity it may open up for you. Or you can choose numerous negative responses, including going crazy which, unfortunately, some people do.

Sometimes a boss or a friend or a spouse can be very upsetting. Dad has a good way of coping when some business problem or client starts driving him up the wall. He talks it over with me then says, "What difference will this make five years from now?" Viewed from that perspective, the frustration dissipates quickly. You needn't allow anyone or anything to remain a problem to you. In fact, you shouldn't! It's not good for you.

Not even God pleases everybody all the time, so why should you expect to? Don't try. Just do the best you can and everything will work out all right. If your reason for doing something is good, the result will be good. Question yourself, and answer truthfully. Doing things for the wrong reasons will destroy your self-esteem and, in time, render you ineffective. You'll know you're on the right track when you feel at peace with yourself, no matter how displeased someone else may be about it. That's their problem. Yours is to stay on course following your own star.

If you start tensing up over someone or something, take some slow, deep breaths, and try to blank the negative thoughts out of your mind. A long walk in the fresh air is a great brain cleanser. The idea is to divert your attention totally away from your problem. Seek out a movie or some other pleasant distraction. Then, when you're ready to think about it again, a good solution is likely to pop right into your head.

Anytime you approach a job hating it, the job will give you fits—like a dog will snarl at you if it senses you don't like it. Maybe you can find something funny about the assignment or figure out a unique approach to it. Suddenly, then, it's a challenge instead of a pain in the neck. If you think, "Oh, I can't do that," you likely won't because you've talked yourself out of succeeding before you've even tried. But if you say, "I wonder if this might work—or that," you may astonish yourself with the results. You're *always* potentially better than you suspect!

When dealing with someone whom you find irritating, play a game with yourself; try to find something likable about him or her (this may take some persistence). After you have uncovered one tolerable trait, see whether there's still another. Before you know it, you will have stopped dwelling on the person's bad points enough that you may even like him, or at least find him tolerable enough to deal with.

It's when life looks blackest that you can be sure something wonderful is about to happen: You and So and So broke up; you're devastated. Mr. Right surfaced, proving that So and So had been Mr. Wrong all the while. See? Without the bad, the good couldn't have occurred.

Your boss promised you a small raise—just enough to enable you to buy a new used car. But business soured and bossman had to postpone your raise. No way can you afford the payments. What alternative have you but to look for other work? Lo and behold, you're exactly what Mr. Zilch needs for his company at double your present salary. How would you have learned how valuable you are had not calamity thrust it upon you?

And so forth. Get it? Trouble creates opportunities. You need it to make progress. Who needs self-pity when better things are in the making?

"Yeah, I feel great!" will get your day off to a better start than, "Bleah, I feel rotten," don't you agree? In fancier language, that's autohypnosis.

The person with the positive attitude will not mind going the extra mile to do his best and not just goof off. Whenever you can make things better or easier for someone else, that's contagious. Why, think how much cleaner public places would be if each person who noticed some litter would pick up two pieces—one for himself and one for the person who threw it there. In time, even the litterers might catch a better attitude.

Gratitude is the only way to keep attitude in shape. The thanks that one feels is a magnet that draws good people and good things toward him or her. Without it, a person could have the moon on a platter and still feel miserable. It's the thanks that adds the joy.

Dad and I have given a lot of thanks for you!

THE SECOND I WALK THROUGH THAT DOOR, I'M GOING TO TURN INTO A FIVE-YEAR-OLD. ...MY MOTHER WILL TREAT ME LIKE A FIVE-YEAR-OLD, FEED ME LIKE A HORSE AND THEN TELL ME MY PANTS ARE TOO TIGHT.

MY PANTS ARE TOO TIGHT... MY HAIR'S TOO LONG... MY NAILS ARE TOO SHORT... MY APARTMENT'S TOO SMALL... MY SKIN IS A MESS... AND THEN SHE'LL SAY I'M PERFECT.

MY MOTHER WILL SAY I'M **SO** PERFECT THAT NO MAN IN THE WORLD IS GOOD ENOUGH FOR ME, AND THEN SHE'LL ASK ME WHY I'M NOT DATING ANYONE.

I KNOW I'LL FEEL PICKED OVER. I KNOW I'LL FEEL GRILLED. I KNOW I'M MARCHING INTO THE ARMS OF THE ONE PERSON WHO CAN MAKE ME GO BERSERK WITH ONE TEENSY GLANCE...

...HOW IRONIC THAT AS I FACE THIS GREAT CHALLENGE, THERE'S ONLY ONE THING I CAN SAY....

MOMMY!!!